Whi

Antisemitis

A collection of submissions made by
individuals to The Chakrabarti Inquiry on
antisemitism and other forms of racism

Edited by Judith Ornstein

Kitty Hawk Press Ltd

Whitewashed

First published Great Britain 2017

By Kitty Hawk Press Ltd

whitewashed@kittyhawkpress.co.uk

Thank you to all the publishers, journals and authors
included here for generously giving us permission to
share your work.
Thanks also to the talented Jilly Lester who drew the
Kitty Hawk logo

A catalogue record for this book
Is available from the British Library
ISBN 978-1-78808-976-0

CONTENTS

3

Statement

The Whitewashed Project, which includes a film and a book, has been produced and self-financed by a group of individuals.

We do not think enough has been done by the Labour Party to root out antisemitism in its midst. There is much misunderstanding, in particular about the relationship between hostility to Israel and antisemitism. Too often those who are concerned about the issue are misrepresented as people who are driven by hostility to the Palestinians or to the left; we say there should be no contradiction between opposing antisemitism, being for Israeli-Palestinian peace, and being on the left. We urge you to watch the film and read the book in order to find out for yourselves why so many Jews in today's Britain are bewildered, frightened and also angry about this unique prejudice.

Oliver Anisfeld
David Hirsh
Judith & Ged Ornstein
Owen Power
Jennie Ross

INTRODUCTION Part 1
Judith Ornstein

In this anthology you will read testimonies submitted by individuals to the Chakrabarti Inquiry into antisemitism and other forms of racism, report published June 30 2016.

They are from all sorts of people, some academic, some not so, some Jewish and some not, and not all UK born. Most of the contributors are deeply committed to the Labour movement.

Each is excellent, but taken together they stand as a powerful witness to what it's been like this last few years to see antisemitism apparently unchecked from the very top of the Labour Party. Antisemitism will never be eradicated but this incarnation can be traced to an early left wing British conspiracy theorist who wrote for the Guardian and who inspired Lenin:

"When Lenin came to write his own thesis on the subject, at Zurich in the spring of 1916, he complained of a shortage of books.
'However,' he wrote, 'I made use of the principal English work on imperialism, J.A. Hobson's book" (Paul Johnson's A History of the Jews. See extract for more evidence)

By ignoring antisemitism, by denying it, not just to us but to themselves, people on the left are condoning antisemitism and this is a new and frightening experience for me; for most Jewish citizens of the UK; and also for many clear sighted non-Jewish people.

Included, to more fully bear witness, are contributions from people who wrote about the aftermath. Howard Jacobson submitted to the report and wrote an analysis in October 2016 calling the Chakrabarti Report 'stillborn'. This was just after the House of Commons Home Affairs Committee on antisemitism had published their report and inter alia made it clear that the Chakrabarti Report is 'compromised'. An extract from the HoC report is included here. And Mark Gardner of the CST gives an eye witness account of the sorry events at the launch.

As I write this introduction in June 2017 we are in the aftermath of a general election where extreme left wingers Jeremy Corbyn, John McDonnnell, Seamus Milne and their acolytes led a Labour Party that won a vastly increased popular vote. The analyses are being churned out. Whatever this election was about, what is obvious is that antisemitism was, at best, irrelevant to masses of British voters.

Together with this book is a documentary film containing interviews with writers of individual submissions. It was made with J-TV and you can view in online through J-TV - YouTube. Each person was asked three questions:
1. What inspired you to write your submission?
2. What did you say?
3. Do you think Shami took any notice?

I don't think it's giving you a spoiler if I ask you to guess the completely unanimous answer to number 3.

I am not Party political but am a believer in social justice. Until recently, the last person to be inspired to produce a political book and documentary, or to know how to do it was me. My beloved mother at 99 told me before she died last year that only when times are at their worst does everyone start talking politics.

Recuperating at home from a serious illness I repeatedly watched John Mann MP whilst he dramatically tackled Ken Livingstone who refused to take back his declaration that Hitler supported Zionism. For his pains John Mann was inundated by antisemitic abuse and calls that he should be expelled from the Labour Party. I set up a social media group in support of John Mann and it turned into a political education.

On April 5 2017 Ken Livingstone, despite being found guilty of bringing Labour into disrepute, was suspended and not expelled from the

Labour Party. He can still vote on party matters and attend meetings.

It felt and still feels, as though the world I know, my England, my Great Britain, my United Kingdom, which I love and which gave my grandparents sanctuary from oppression, has been replaced by a country I no longer recognise and which does not value its Jewish minority. This is particularly prevalent in the Labour Party. Social media groups are full of distressed Jewish Labour supporter from way back who now have no political home. These groups are also full of Jewish people of all political persuasions seriously considering whether our time in this country is up.

Despite what many people believe, the patient must be worth saving. There are good people in this country of political party allegiance and none, and many of them are Labour Party supporters whose voices are not being heard.

Thank you to each contributor for sharing with a stranger when I put out the call. From Shami, not one of you received more than a computer generated acknowledgment for your submission;   your thoughtful, literate, knowledgeable and passionate writing seemed doomed to oblivion. Richard Gold's ending sticks with me:

"Writing this report is demeaning, it feels as if I have to grovel to simply play a part in getting the Labour Party to combat the problem of anti-Semitism. This shouldn't be needed, Jews shouldn't have to feel like this, in the Labour Party of 2016".

How even more demeaning to feel that your voices, representing so many of us in what David Hirsh calls the democratic consensus among Jews and non- Jews , have still not been listened to. I hope we have honoured you as you should have been from the beginning.

Acknowledgments
1. Not one person who submitted as an individual to Chakrabarti is named or acknowledged on the report itself.

Chakrabarti has claimed this was for reasons of confidentiality. Each contributor to this project was asked about any correspondence,

11

relating to confidentiality or anything at all. Some people are clear that they received no acknowledgment at all. Most people received only the following computer generated acknowledgement:

"Thank you for emailing the Chakrabarti Inquiry. Please do not reply to this email. This email is to acknowledge that the Inquiry has received your email. We apologise for not being able to provide individual acknowledgements of responses to the Inquiry due to the volume of responses. This email is regularly monitored and all responses received by 10 June 2016 will be considered.

Sent by email from the Labour Party, promoted by Iain McNicol on behalf of The Labour Party, both at Southside, 105 Victoria Street, London, SW1E 6QT Website: www.labour.org.uk to join or renew call 0345 092 2299."

The exception is Ric Cooper who asked some questions and received a different computer generated acknowledgment:

Received 27 May 2016: "Dear Mr Cooper, Thank you for your email, which has been passed on to Ms Chakrabarti for her to consider. Due to the volume of responses to the inquiry it may not be possible for the inquiry to enter into further dialogue with you, Yours sincerely, Godric Jolliffe, Solicitor to the Chakrabarti Inquiry"

I do not believe that Shami Chakrabarti deliberately set out to whitewash allegations of antisemitism within elements of the Labour Party.   Because of her exemplary record in campaigning for human rights, the people who wrote these submissions hoped that this report would offer an independent critique and solution. She failed to acknowledge adequately their heartfelt submissions, or ask if she might quote from them. The Inquiry was launched on 29th April 2016 and the report published on 30th June 2016 with its remit broadened to include 'Antisemitism and other forms of Racism'. The speed of the inquiry and Shami Chakrabarti's acceptance of a peerage in the immediate aftermath added to a perception that the issue of antisemitism was not, and has still not, been sufficiently dealt with.

Thank you to the young talented and inspiring Ollie Anisfeld and J-TV for taking on this project. Thank you to the brilliant and impassioned fighter against antisemitism , David Hirsh for deciding to trust me even though you didn't then know me from Adam, but you came on board with the project. Together with my darling husband Ged we've challenged each other, and collaborated as a great team.

Thanks too to dear Owen Power and Jennie Ross for your loyal and generous support, your faith in the project, and for keeping me calm.

I urge you to read this anthology and to watch the film with an open mind, wherever you are in time, geography and politics.

INTRODUCTION Part 2
David Hirsh

In the spring of 2016, the Labour Party judged that it had a problem with antisemitism which needed addressing. Jeremy Corbyn asked Shami Chakrabarti to lead an inquiry.

This volume is a collection of some of the documents that people sat down to write in order to try and help Chakrabarti understand the issue and move towards solutions. When the report was published, these people felt, broadly, that Chakrabarti had failed to do what needed to be done to address the problem.

There had always been antisemitism in dusty and obsessive corners of the Labour movement but Jeremy Corbyn's emergence as leader was symbolic of the shift of this kind of politics into the mainstream.

The submissions to Chakrabarti tried to help the inquiry by offering insight on the difficult relationships between hostility to Israel, support for the Palestinians, and antisemitism. Everybody agrees that criticism of Israel is not antisemitic; but when everything is considered as 'criticism' and nothing is admitted to be antisemitism, there is a problem. The submissions tried to give Chakrabarti an idea of what it is like to be Jewish in today's Labour Party.

The submissions situated the current problem of antisemitism as being related to the leadership of Jeremy Corbyn. It wasn't so much that he himself was responsible for it; but he had been part of this kind of politics for his whole career; he legitimized it; and he showed himself time and again unable to make the distinction between criticism of Israel and antisemitism. It turned out that Shami Chakrabarti was not a neutral judge; she was on Team Corbyn and she produced a report which did more to make the questions go away than to answer them.

Many thought that just Corbyn's work for the Iranian propaganda TV station disqualified him from leadership; or just the fact that he had said that Hamas and Hezbollah were dedicated to peace and justice; or that he supported a boycott of Israel but nowhere else on the planet; or the fact that he jumped to the defence of blood libeller Raed Salah or conspiracy theorist Steven Sizer, defending them against a charge of antisemitism. Any one of a hundred things seemed to make Corbyn unsuited to lead the Labour Party.

Many Labour supporters assumed that somebody with this record could not be a serious candidate for Prime Minister and they opposed Corbyn because they wanted a Labour Prime Minister. But it turns out that a person with this record can, in the age of populism, be a serious candidate. After the June 2017 General Election, Corbyn's leadership looks unassailable and suddenly even many of his opponents in the party are putting their shoulders to his wheel, keeping their heads down and hoping Corbyn will bring them into government on his coat tails.

But the issue of antisemitism will not go away. Antisemitism is a threat to Jews but it also a threat to democratic politics. It has always been an indicator of a deeper political sickness.

17

Some will say that it is now disloyal to talk about Corbyn's relationship to antisemitism; some will continue to teach Labour activists to recognise talk about antisemitism as a marker of Zionist bad faith or of Tory smears.

We are publishing these submissions to the Chakrabarti Inquiry in the hope that they will help people to understand that there is a real issue here; it should not be mis-recognized as bullying lies made by political opponents. We hope that people will read the submissions and that they will feed into rational thinking on this topic. Angry denial and counter-accusations will not do.

Let's be clear – antisemitism is a hate apart
Howard Jacobson
First published The Guardian October 23 2016

To the question posed by the parliamentary committee last week, as to whether Shami Chakrabarti's soft enquiry into antisemitism in the Labour Party was a whitewash for which Corbyn brazenly rewarded her with a peerage, or evidence of a deep seated reluctance to take the subject seriously, there is unlikely to be a satisfactory answer. Where people are convinced of their own rectitude - and Corbyn and Chakrabarti belong to the more unself-questioning wing of British politics - there is no separating what they know from what they don't want to know.

The Chakrabarti Enquiry didn't fail, it was stillborn. Corbyn has always defended himself against the charge of antisemitism by protesting his freedom from all racisms - an insistence that feels like an evasion and blurs a crucial distinction - and the moment Chakrabarti widened the terms of her enquiry likewise, there was no hope for it.

To assert that antisemitism is unlike other racisms is not to claim a privilege for it. Hating a Jew is no worse than hating anyone else. But while many a prejudice is set off by particular circumstance - the rise in an immigrant population, or a locally perceived threat - antisemitism is as often as not unprompted, exists outside time and place, and doesn't even require the presence of Jews to explain it. When Marlowe and Shakespeare responded to an appetite for anti-Jewish feeling in Elizabethan England, there had been no Jews in the country for 300 years. Jewishness, for its enemies, is as much an idea as it is anything else.

The part played by Jews in the evolution of Christianity has much to do with this. In the popular imagination the Jew is the killer of Christ. To a philosopher like Nietzsche the Jew is culpable not for rejecting Christianity but for inventing it. For cultures unable to make up their minds whether they are heathen or Christian - remember those demonstrations of Teutonic paganism on the streets of Christian Germany eighty years ago - the Jew fits the bill of villain twice.

If the Jew transmogrified into the devil for the Medieval church, he retained his devilish characteristics as Christian sentiment found other places to express itself, early socialism being one of them. Weighted down with his Judas moneybags, rootless, usurious, conspiratorial, and believing himself to be 'chosen', the Jew glided seamlessly into the demonology of the Left. Not always, it should be said, without his own connivance. Many Jews have found one or other version of socialism compatible with their religious faith, while others have been quick to embrace a secular system in whose name they can jettison that faith altogether. The presence of a Jew in any movement no more guarantees it to be innocent of antisemitism than guilty. And that applies to anti-Zionism too. Anti-Zionist Jews exist, but that tells one nothing about anti-Zionism.

21

It is here, anyway, in the matter of the existence of the State of Israel, that all the ancient superstitions about Jews find a point of confluence. We dance around this subject afraid to confront it full on. But it has to be addressed: partly because all that has been thought about Jews in the past has a home in what we think about Israel now, and partly because it is axiomatic to Labour that Zionism is a racist ideology - from which it follows that anti-Zionism cannot be called racist - we will not fix antisemitism, in the Labour Party or anywhere else, until we fix Israel. I don't mean fix its problems, I mean fix the way we talk about it.

The mantra bedevilling reasonable conversation about Israel is that the Jews have only one motive in labelling anti-Zionism antisemitic, and that is to stifle legitimate criticism of Israel. This assertion defames Jews, the majority of whom, in my experience, take issue, not with the idea of legitimate criticism, but with what in any given instance 'legitimacy' amounts to. Criticism is not an inviolable concept. It can be moderate or extreme, truthful or mendacious, well-intentioned or malign. To complain when it is unjust is not to shut down debate. It cannot be exorbitant to argue that what will determine whether criticism of Israel is antisemitic is the nature of the criticism.

The effect of a libel is to exhaust trust. It should not be automatically assumed that when it comes to Israel Jews are incapable of arguing honestly - an assumption which itself edges dangerously close to the racism that's being denied. We need to separate this from that. No, 'legitimate' (that is to say fair and honest) criticism of Israel as a nation among nations does not amount to antisemitism. Anti-Zionism, on the other hand - the repudiation of Israel's right to exist - almost invariably does.

Zionism originated as a liberation movement. It grew out of an urgent concern, voiced by nineteenth century Jews and Gentiles alike, for the safety and well-being of Jews, and concluded that only if they had their own country would the deracinated Jews of Europe and elsewhere, including the Middle East, be free from discrimination and persecution. To deny its necessity, whatever its subsequent disappointments and betrayals, is to deny history. Zionism took many forms, but neither conquest nor colonial expansionism was one of them. If anything, Zionism was marked by a dreamy not to say Utopian idealism. Jews would return to the land and work hand in hand with their Arab brethren in an amity that would benefit them both. Not all Jews believed it would work. The world didn't need another nationalism, internationalists argued. True, Jews had suffered at the hands of everybody else's, and it was bad luck on them if lifeboats were to be declared illegitimate just as it was their turn to jump, but history can be cruel. It got a little crueller later, and many a critic of Zionism was forced to eat his words when the death camps emptied.

Is that me playing the Holocaust card? Maybe Jeremy Corbyn and Baroness Chakrabarti would think so. Maybe their rooted suspicion of Jewish motives explains the paltriness of Chakrabarti's report and the insolence of Corbyn's refusal to take any criticism of it on board. But the more the Labour Party puts its fingers in its ears, the greater the perception of its deafness will become. We need to talk about Zion.

Eye Witness at the Launch of the
Chakrabarti Inquiry Report
Mark Gardner
Director of Communications, CST

The 30 June 2016 launch event for Shami
Chakrabarti's Inquiry report into antisemitism,
could have given a much needed morale boost
for those seeking assurance that the Labour
Party was understanding, or at least hearing,
the fears and experiences of British Jews.
Instead, the circus around Jeremy Corbyn
ensured that the opposite happened.

The launch event was Corbyn's opportunity to
directly address the issue of antisemitism and
the collapse of Jewish confidence in Labour,
but it was instead a rally against his enemies
of the moment, specifically the media and his
opponents within Labour. Worse still, the
lasting publicity from the launch was that Ruth
Smeeth MP (Labour) had left it in tears, due to
what she perceived as antisemitic hectoring
from a known Corbyn ally, who had accused
her and the Daily Telegraph of "working hand
in hand."

I attended the launch event with colleagues from CST and other Jewish communal organisations. We had done our utmost to constructively assist Shami Chakrabarti, trying assiduously to explain how and why mainstream Jews were feeling increasingly repelled by both antisemitism and hysterical anti-Zionism in the Party. We did this because it seemed a critical juncture in the relationship between Jews and Labour, and despite - or perhaps due to - our deep reservations about why Corbyn had commissioned the Inquiry, following two previous antisemitism investigations by Labour Students and Baroness Jan Royall.

The atmosphere before the launch was highly fraught. Corbyn was enduring a post-Brexit hammering, but our concern was fully focused upon Chakrabarti's report. None of us knew its content, and we had heatedly discussed what success and failure might look like. Nobody from Labour had worked with the community to ensure it had some kind of buy-in to the launch event, but we did not expect the launch itself to be the story, the latest vicious spin in our relationship with the leadership of the Labour Party.

Things went wrong from the start. Entering the venue in Savoy Place, Corbyn supporters were there in numbers. For them, the report was meaningless, as revealed when some of them asked us if we knew what room "the rally" would be in. Next, in the room itself, Corbyn's supporters were handing out leaflets against "traitors" (the same word used two weeks previously by the murderer of Jo Cox MP). It was inexplicable and disgraceful why such leafletting was being allowed. Corbyn's Director of Strategy and Communications Seumas Milne stood at the back.

This was not a sombre room, awaiting the verdict of an independent adjudicator on whether or not a leading political party had succumbed to racism. The gathering storm burst into full applause when Corbyn entered, alongside Chakrabarti. The mood was verging on triumphant. Corbyn sat immediately in front of me and this room was his, not ours, nor that of an independent inquiry into the party he was leading. The report had been handed out and I tried hard to focus on it, but could not stop thinking that this was the closest I had ever come to experiencing a personality cult.

To be clear, Corbyn was not the subject of Chakrabarti's Inquiry, but for many Jews he personified the problems that they expressed to her, the fears that they trusted her with. So, Chakrabarti's double act with Corbyn (which would quickly double down and triple down in subsequent media and select committee appearances) struck all of the wrong notes, betraying all notion of independent scrutiny. It further emboldened his supporters in the room, so that with each passing minute, the actual content and purpose of the report became increasingly irrelevant.
In a tone of calm determination, Corbyn delivered a fully prepared speech that revealed he knew what was in this supposedly independent report. Those not there to venerate him audibly gasped when he said that Jews should not be blamed for the actions of Israel, just as Muslims should not be blamed for the actions of "self-styled Islamic States or organisations."

29

When later asked if he had meant to equate Israel to ISIS, Corbyn firmly denied it, but it was very hard to shake the suspicion that he (or his speech writer) had deliberately not said "Muslim countries", a far more obvious and neutral wording.

If, despite all of the above, Corbyn had merely accepted the report's findings, condemned antisemitism, and departed the building after declining media questions (exactly as he had done the day before when visiting a Polish centre), then we might, perhaps, have been able to try and move forward: but what happened next became the abiding headline from the launch.

Chakrabarti chaired proceedings, choosing which of the many journalists could ask questions. Notably, the gathered UK Jewish media were not even invited to ask a single question. So, the questioning concentrated upon Corbyn's leadership struggles and side-lined the communal media that a sincere anti-racist event would have tried to reach, or at least include.

When asked by a Daily Telegraph journalist to condemn the wording of the "traitors" leaflet that his supporters had distributed at the event, Corbyn did so, plainly and forcefully, stressing his belief in a kinder form of politics. Then, Marc Wadsworth, one of the leaflet distributors, accused Ruth Smeeth MP, who was sitting nearby him, of working "hand in hand" with the Telegraph. Ruth Smeeth is Jewish, but this ought not to define her, as she is also a proud, longstanding anti-racist campaigner and Labour Party activist in her own right. She left the room in tears, a Jewish Labour MP driven out by the atmosphere of bullying brought about by Corbyn's supporters, believing that Wadsworth had voiced an antisemitic conspiracy tying her with Corbyn's media opponents. This sorry scene exemplified how much the preceding months had meant to opponents of antisemitism and how cruelly their hopes had been shattered.

After that, the postscript seemed entirely fitting, with Corbyn filmed leaving the room whilst chatting amicably to Wadsworth. The politics of hypocrisy and intimidation had been allowed to overwhelm a potentially key moment in the struggle against contemporary antisemitism. It proved, yet again, that supposedly universal rules of anti-racism, basic decency and respect, are not applied to mainstream Jewish concerns and sensitivities. Until that culture is recognised and changed from within, it is hard to see how Jews can ever be ordinary, normal, unremarkable, equal members of the Labour Party.

Luke Akehurst's submission
sets out the ways in which activists use
language and images that are drawn from
historic antisemitic tropes that were
previously applied to Jews per se, and use
them to attack the only Jewish State.

Dear Shami,

I am writing as a Labour Party member of 28
years standing and former NEC member,
councillor and parliamentary candidate.

I thought it would be useful to submit to your
inquiry the piece I wrote about antisemitism
for Labourlist in April:

I declare an interest in that I am not Jewish
but I'm a Zionist (literally meaning someone
who supports Jewish national self-
determination through the creation and
existence of a Jewish State in Israel) and my
day job is running a pro-Israel campaign group,
We Believe in Israel, so I am very conscious of
where the boundary lies between legitimate
criticism of Israel and antisemitism.

33

It's apparent from the reactions to the recent cases in the Labour Party that many people in the party are unaware of or in denial that antisemitism (prejudice and hatred towards Jewish people) can exist as a left phenomenon, and if they do accept it, confused about which aspects of extreme anti-Israel rhetoric are offensive.

It's easy for people on the left to understand the reality of far right antisemitism because we are all familiar (or should be) with the history of the rise to power of the Nazis and the Holocaust. It makes sense to us as leftists because clearly the Nazis were a common enemy to both Jews and socialists and that the same goes for modern day neo-Nazis like the BNP.

Things get a bit more difficult with religious/cultural antisemitism. This isn't something that makes sense to most of us on the left because our own secular values mean we often don't have much knowledge of these phenomena. But it doesn't take much study to discover there are deep undercurrents of antisemitism in both Christian history (the concept of the Jews as killers of Christ and the idea in "replacement theology" that they therefore lost God's covenant and were replaced by the Christian church) which drove pogroms from the Middle Ages onward; and in Muslim history (negative references to Jews in the Koran, dhimmis restrictions on Jews living under Muslim rule, and in extreme Islamist thinking, e.g. the Hamas charter, overt calls to kill Jews). Of course, most people who are contemporary followers of these religions don't buy into these views, but a minority do.

But most of us on the left are blissfully ignorant of the long history of antisemitism in our own ranks. We like to delude ourselves that we are pure, and good, and incapable of racism. But sadly there's a long history of prejudice and hatred towards Jews on the left, and no tradition is immune from it. In the orthodox Communist tradition Stalin was notoriously and overtly antisemitic, promoting wild conspiracy theories about Zionists and "rootless cosmopolitan" Jews, which given his propensity to have people shot or deported to the Gulag, often had a lethal effect.

35

Some groups in the Trotskyist tradition have employed antisemitic imagery. On Labour's right, Ernie Bevin, a man I would otherwise see as my hero because of his role founding the TGWU union, NATO and the British nuclear deterrent, handled the crisis in Mandatory Palestine that led to Israel's creation with ill-disguised antisemitic prejudice towards the Jews.

I don't know the extent of antisemitic views within the Labour Party. I don't think the cases so far are likely to be the end of it. I think the rhetoric around the Israel/Palestinian conflict has become so inflamed and black and white in recent years that a significant number of people both from the hard left and Labour people whose values are informed by particular versions of Christian or Muslim thinking have started to cross the line between anti-Zionism and antisemitism. The leadership election last year brought many people from a far left milieu into or back into the Labour Party and it is simple fact that the prevalence of antisemitic versions of anti-Zionism is higher the further left you go.

But even if it was just half a dozen cases, that's half a dozen too many to tolerate in a party dedicated to equality and anti-racism, and half a dozen more than the reputation of our party and all the noble things it stands for and has done can stand the stain of.

The contemporary debate about Israel is a difficult area because Israel is both at the heart of a complex conflict with the Palestinians, which is one of the most contentious issues in global politics, with contradictory national narratives on each side; and it's the world's only Jewish State, perceived by the vast majority of Jews globally as being the fulfilment of aspirations to national liberation, a lifeboat that secures the Jewish people against any repeat of the Holocaust, and somewhere Jews feel a deep cultural, family and religious connection to.

There are many political activists – including many Zionists – who are able to criticise Israeli policies and politicians, to oppose the occupation of the West Bank, the building of settlements, or the manner in which Israel has

37

conducted military operations in Gaza, using language that does not cause distress to Jews.

There are some political activists – including some Jews – who are anti-Zionists in the sense that they think a Jewish State is a mistake and they want to persuade Israeli Jews towards a one state solution with the Palestinians, and manage the more difficult political balancing act of doing this using language that does not cause distress to Jews (it's quite difficult not to distress people when you are urging them to forego their right to national self-determination, unless you are an anarchist or communist and deny the concept of nation states full-stop, not just for the Jews. If you are denying self-determination to Jews and want the only Jewish state gone the onus is really on you to explain why that isn't antisemitic as the result is deeply offensive to most Jews.). As the Community Security Trust (CST), the British Jewish Community's charity for tackling antisemitism says "Not all anti-Zionists are antisemites and anti-Zionism is not necessarily antisemitic."

By the way, if you don't think antisemitism is a real threat today, please explain why Jewish schools and synagogues have to be guarded by CST volunteers.

Perhaps the best approach to testing whether your rhetoric on Israel is antisemitic is to put yourself in the shoes of a Jewish person and try to think how they would feel about the remarks that have been attributed to the various people recently suspended by the Labour Party, and other discourse on social media. Which of them would you find offensive or hurtful? Which of them would make you think the person making them was prejudiced against you as a Jew, not just Israel as a state? It was established by the MacPherson report that the most important thing when looking at allegations of racism is to understand how the victim perceives the case. The All Party Parliamentary Inquiry into Antisemitism said "We take into account the view expressed in the Macpherson report of the Stephen Lawrence Inquiry that a racist act is defined by its victim. It is not acceptable for an individual to say 'I am not a racist' if his or her words or acts are perceived to be racist. We conclude that it is the Jewish community itself that is best qualified to determine what does and does not constitute antisemitism."

The easiest examples are when former Woking parliamentary candidate Vicki Kirby talked about Jews having "big noses" and when Luton councillor Aysegul Gurbuz's Twitter feed praised Hitler as the "greatest man in history". It should be fairly obvious these are examples of antisemitism.

But antisemitism can also come into the debate about Israel when people use language and images that are drawn from historic antisemitic tropes that were previously applied to Jews *per se*, and use them to attack the only Jewish State:
Claims of Jewish or Zionist conspiracy theories, Jewish or Zionist control of the media, finance and political processes, for instance saying Israel controls Isis or Israel controls US or British foreign policy. This sort of stuff is straight out of the "Protocols of the Elders of Zion", a forgery produce by Tsarist secret police.

Claims that British Jews have a dual loyalty that means they are more loyal to Israel than to the country they are citizens of.
Allegations that Israel is acting like the Nazis, that events in Gaza or the West Bank constitute a Holocaust, that Gaza is a concentration camp. This is Holocaust Inversion – telling the Jews who were the victims of the Holocaust that they are the new Nazis. I can't think of anything more grotesque. These Nazi analogies are deeply hurtful to all Jews and designed to cause maximum distress.

Substitution on placards at demos or on social media memes of swastikas for Stars of David. As CST's Dave Rich said last year "Don't you find it odd that the only political demonstrations where it is considered OK by people on the Left to wave a swastika, just happen to be protests against the world's only Jewish state? That's an almighty coincidence." Use of language such as "baby killers" to describe Israeli military actions, when this has echoes of the Blood Libel, the mediaeval Christian myth that Jews killed gentile babies to use their blood to make Passover matzo bread, which was often used as the catalyst to start pogroms.

Denial of Jewish peoplehood and historical connection to Israel – including the allegation that Ashkenazi (European) Jews have no genetic connection to Middle Eastern Jews and are not "real Jews" but stem from some mass conversion in the Dark Ages.

Use of Zionism, Zionist and "Zio" not to describe simple belief in Jewish rights to a state but as an insult implying conspiratorial power and evil intent (exactly mirroring traditional antisemitic images of Jews).

Dehumanising and demonising language that was historically used against Jews being deployed against Israel and Zionists e.g. "bacteria, rats, cancer, plague".

Signalling out Zionism and Israel as uniquely illegitimate when you don't target any other forms of national movement or country.

Just swapping the word Zionist in instead of Jew isn't a get out clause for using old-fashioned antisemitic tropes. As CST say: "Employing the word 'Zionist' where the word

'Jew' would have previously appeared in open antisemitic discourse may, or may not, be deliberate obfuscation on the part of the user. Nevertheless, it essentially fulfils the same psychological and political purpose as open antisemitism once did."

Some harsh and unfair criticism of Israel is not antisemitic. I hate the attempts to compare Israel to apartheid South Africa. Professor Alan Johnson has comprehensively rebutted this smear. But whilst it is an unfair allegation, and I will fight it politically because it is part of an effort to delegitimise Israel, it isn't an inherently antisemitic one.

I expect people to advocate passionately for the Palestinians and to have heartfelt criticisms of Israel.

But if you find yourself discussing Israel using images or language that could just as easily come from a Nazi or Stalinist or Tsarist antisemitic pamphlet, and that are likely to cause your Jewish fellow citizens to feel distress or even fearful, you have crossed a line. And you definitely don't belong in a modern democratic socialist party that prides itself on anti-racism.

Yours sincerely,
Luke Akehurst

Joint Submission

Jonathan G Campbell Senior Lecturer in Biblical Studies & Judaism, University of Bristol and

Lesley D Klaff (Senior Lecturer in Law, Sheffield Hallam University)

explain the relationship between the Labour Party's hostility to Israel and antisemitism, and the relationship between Israel and Jewish identity

As academics with interests in the study of contemporary antisemitism, we would be grateful if the inquiry would take into account the following two interrelated points:

1. The Labour Party cannot honestly hold itself out as "an anti-racist party committed to combating and campaigning against all forms of racism, including antisemitism....." as long as it denies the existence of left-wing antisemitism within the Party. Left-wing antisemitism takes the form of irrational,

45

disproportionate, and stereotyped hostility to Israel, treating the country in effect as the 'Jew among nations'. It involves an intellectual discourse which conceives of Israel in partial and distorted form and employs a conceptual framework that is both false and falsifying. This includes claims that Zionism is racism; that Israel's creation involved the ethnic cleansing of the indigenous people of Palestine; that Israel is a settler-colonial state which is now committing genocide against the Palestinians; and that all Israeli defensive action is disproportionate or unnecessary. The discourse similarly draws on the belief in an all-powerful Israel lobby and on nasty and provocative comparisons of Israel with apartheid South Africa and/or the Nazis. Further, left-wing antisemitism is at the heart of a global social movement, the BDS movement, which aims to remove Israel from the world stage in complete disregard of the perfectly legitimate needs and wishes of the roughly six million Israeli Jews who live there. This desire to see Israel's demise constitutes contemporary anti-Zionism. Such anti-Zionism was officially given a definition in 2002 by the Berlin Technical University's Centre for

Research on Antisemitism, which it drafted for the European Union Monitoring Centre for Research on Racism and Xenophobia. It defines anti-Zionism as "the portrayal of Israel as a state that is fundamentally negatively distinct from all others and which therefore has no right to exist."

2. Contemporary anti-Zionism as described above is antisemitic. It applies double standards to the world's only Jewish state in order to demonise and delegitimize it so as to justify its removal from the community of nations. It also often transfers classic antisemitic notions about alleged Jewish power and malice to the state of Israel alone of all countries in the world. This is inevitably painful for most British Jews, the overwhelming majority of whom have an affinity with Israel and the Zionist project, so much so that Israel and Zionism are a key aspect of contemporary Jewish identity in the UK, broadly comparable to the place of the Irish Republic in the identity of Irish Americans. Accordingly, the majority of British Jews assume a certain obligation to support Israel and to ensure its survival as the

47

ancestral homeland of the Jewish people. This does not equate to unconditional or unstinting support for any particular Israeli government and its policies. Rather, it amounts to a sense of connection with, or an affiliation to, modern Israel, as well as a sense of the country's importance against the background of historic Jewish ties to the land, the persecution of Jews over the ages, and the renewed opportunity since 1922 (with the creation of British Palestine as the Jewish National Home) and especially since 1948 (with the formation of the state of Israel) for Jewish self-determination and cultural flourishing. For these reasons, left-wing hostility to Israel engages Jews not only in conventional political terms but also seeks to undermine a perfectly respectable core aspect of their identity. Nor is the existence of a small group of Jews who are hostile to Israel and Zionism evidence for the proposition that an attachment to Israel is not an important aspect of contemporary Jewish identity, for such Jews are either marginal or non-normative or, paradoxically, the form that their attachment to Israel takes is in their hostility to Israel and Zionism.

These two points are vital to understanding antisemitism in the modern Labour Party, for the grossly inaccurate discourse about Israel that they entail seems endemic to large sections of the Party at present, especially since Jeremy Corbyn became leader. The general demonization of Israel that results inevitably creates a permissive environment in which outrageous statements about Israel or Israeli Jews – or indeed Diaspora Jews with links to Israel – can be made by individual Party members. It may well be appropriate to take disciplinary action against such members, but the real problem lies in the prior permissive environment and its anti-Israel discourse. Without tackling the latter head on, indeed, the Labour Party will not in our view be able to deal thoroughly or successfully with the problem of antisemitism that is currently in its midst.

Ric Cooper 's Submission
Former shopkeeper and property investor,
now part-time archivist, genealogist and
blogger.

This was my submission to the Chakrabarti
Inquiry together with their only
acknowledgement.

As a concerned Jew I am writing to ask for
your response to the following two questions
about the Inquiry into the Labour Party which
you will shortly be chairing:
Can you confirm that you will not be applying
double standards by on the one hand
dismissing the European Union Agency for
Fundamental Rights (FRA) and Pickles
governmental definitions of antisemitism, and
on the other hand giving weight to accusations
of Islamophobia made against those who
merely wish to protest the incitement of
violence?

Can you confirm that you will not be perversely standing Macpherson on its head by accepting the testimony of those Jews who categorise such statements as "the creation of Israel as a Jewish State was a crime" and "Jews of all people should have learnt from the Holocaust to turn the other cheek" as fair comment, and not the antisemitism that they are?

From: Inquiry <inquiry@labour.org.uk>
Date: 27 May 2016 at 17:39
Subject: Re: The Chakrabarti Inquiry
To: Richard Cooper

Dear Mr Cooper
Thank you for your email, which has been passed on to Ms Chakrabarti for her to consider. Due to the volume of responses to the inquiry it may not be possible for the inquiry to enter into further dialogue with you.

Yours sincerely

Godric Jolliffe
Solicitor to the Chakrabarti Inquiry

51

Baroness Ruth Deech's Submission
Ruth Deech examines the failings of the
Chakrabarti Inquiry in relation to
discriminatory practices against Jews and
Israel on British campuses, and calls for the
adoption by universities of the government
and international definition of antisemitism.

The terms of reference of your inquiry are of
initial concern. It was set up in response to
cases of antisemitic statements by members
of the Labour Party. The remit has however
been diluted, and it is not clear on what
authority this has come about. Thus:-

It now includes "and other forms of racism,
including Islamophobia."
There have been no complaints of other forms
of racism or Islamophobia on the part of
members of the Labour Party, so there is no
need to include this.

Moreover, antisemitism is entirely different from other forms of racism and Islamophobia. It is different because of its history going back over millennia, the way in which antisemitism has mutated over the centuries according to the obsessions of the times, whether religious, racial or nationalistic; its association with religious teaching and anti-Jewish preaching on the part of Christianity and Islam. Since the Koran undeniably contains anti-Jewish sentiments, the inclusion of Islamophobia as a concept in the inquiry will shift focus away from that particular root cause of antisemitism.

Above all, the examination of antisemitism is special and difficult because of its association with criticism of Israel and the Zionist movement for Jewish self- determination. There is no parallel in other forms of racism or Islamophobia.

By including racism and Islamophobia, the inquiry may quite readily slide into generalities and avoid facing up to the real causes of antisemitism. Nor will the Jewish community accept that it is sufficient to say that "all forms of racism are unacceptable", as Jeremy Corbyn has stated. Words come more easily than action, and the nature of antisemitism is diluted by wrapping it up with other racisms. The issues relating to Jews and Israel need discrete attention. It is unacceptable and untrue that accusations of antisemitism have been raised recently out of the blue in order to undermine the Labour party; many Jewish people have been aware of the growth of it on the Left for decades. Complaints made in the past have gone unnoticed: it is social media that have brought these incidents to the forefront and made them impossible to overlook. Books that the panel should refer to on this include David Nirenberg, *Anti-Judaism* and Anthony Julius, *Trials of the Diaspora*.

My own experience of antisemitism has not been at the hands of the Labour party, but at school, and more recently by witnessing statements on the part of politicians, including peers, that cross the line from criticism of Israel into antisemitism. I have also been contacted by Jewish students from many universities who have told me about antisemitic incidents affecting them - they contact me because I was from 2004-2008 the first Independent Adjudicator for Higher Education, a statutory post established to act as a final appeal in relation to student complaints that could not be settled locally. I have been informed of incidents at UCL, KCL, LSE, Southampton, Exeter, Warwick, Edinburgh, Glasgow, SOAS, Oxford, Cambridge, and others.

In order to clarify that difficult line between legitimate criticism of a government and antisemitism, it is important that your inquiry adopt the definition of antisemitism that has now been taken up by our government:-

See - https://www.gov.uk/government/speeches/a-definition-of-antisemitism

It is particularly important to draw attention to the government's guidance on when that criticism crosses the line, as set out the government website -

Examples of the ways in which antisemitism manifests itself with regard to the State of Israel taking into account the overall context could include:

Denying the Jewish people their right to self-determination, e.g., by claiming that the existence of a State of Israel is a racist endeavor.

Applying double standards by requiring of it a behavior not expected or demanded of any other democratic nation.

Using the symbols and images associated with classic antisemitism (e.g., claims of Jews killing Jesus or blood libel) to characterize Israel or Israelis.

Drawing comparisons of contemporary Israeli policy to that of the Nazis.

Holding Jews collectively responsible for actions of the state of Israel.

Moreover, the International Holocaust Remembrance Association comprising 31 states, of which the UK is a past chair and current member, has adopted a similar definition and examples set out here:

https://www.holocaustremembrance.com/sites/default/files/press_release_document_antisemitism.pdf

Resistance to these definitions, which may be found on Twitter etc., serve to indicate that the objectors wish to shelter their antisemitic remarks behind criticism of Israel. The objections of an organisation known as "Independent Jewish Voices" should be discounted because a. most of the members only identify as Jews when they wish to avoid opprobrium attaching to Israel, and do not so identify in their daily lives (a stance accurately described by Howard Jacobson in *The Finkler Question*) and b. there is no such thing as a non-independent Jewish voice! The overwhelming majority of Jews see Israel as a vital component of their identity and beliefs. For them, to delegitimise or wish away the land to which they have been attached, and in which Jews have resided, for thousands of years, is most definitely an attack on their religion.

To assist in determining whether a remark or resolution concerning Israel is in fact

57

antisemitic, a useful test is to substitute the name of another country for "Israel". An example would be a state founded in aftermath of the Second World War as a homeland restricted to one ethnic group alone because there was war between that ethnic group and another; that involved the displacement of hundreds of thousands of residents and the deprivation of their property; that is governed by religious law; that has nuclear weapons; that has a poor human rights record; and is in dispute over territory, ie Pakistan.

If a politician were to say that "Pakistan will not be there forever", or "Pakistan is the root of all the problems in the Far East"; "Pakistan should never have come into existence", or "Pakistan is a racist and colonialist endeavour", "Pakistanis in the UK should go back to Pakistan", there would be outrage at this clear expression of racism. If a university were to host "Boycott Pakistan Week", or "Saudi Arabia Misogyny Week" it would be condemned for racial discrimination against students of those origins. But parallel statements have been made, and actions

(Israel Apartheid Week) undertaken in relation to Israel in the guise of legitimate criticism of the state.

Where a party supporter is accused of antisemitism, there should be an inquiry by an independent panel, which should determine guilt, and an independent panel should be reconvened to consider the end of suspension. It is unacceptable that Jackie Walker or Ken Livingstone should be readmitted - by what process is not known - to the Party without any indication of change of heart or mind.

There is also the need for the inquiry to investigate whether those politicians accused of antisemitism were making those statements in a misguided attempt to court their voters. Naz Shah, (and coincidentally, George Galloway, her predecessor as MP, and David Ward, a former Lib-Dem MP, who was suspended from his party for calling for the end of Israel but was recently re-elected as a councillor), represented Bradford. The Census of 2011 revealed that Bradford's population was 24.7% Muslim, no doubt higher by now. There are wards of Bradford, Blackburn and

Burnley (the constituencies of councillors suspended for antisemitic remarks) where the percentage of Muslims is 70%. David Ward's successor as MP, Imran Hussain, has also gone out of his way to criticise Israel. It is not even as subtle as a "dog whistle". These politicians seem to be playing to what they believe to be their Muslim voters' prejudices. A recent Channel 4 TV survey of the attitudes of British Muslims, which may have been of influence, found *inter alia* that 26% of the UK Muslim community believed Jews were responsible for the majority of the world's conflicts, and that 40% of those surveyed believed that UK Jews were more loyal to Israel than to Britain. "Anti-Semitism isn't just tolerated in some sections of the British Muslim community; it's routine and commonplace." (Mehdi Hasan, British Muslim political journalist).

It is arguable that politicians who court thousands of voters who they think may believe this rubbish are now feeling the need to pander to them, rather than think for themselves and stand up against prejudice. That is the real tragedy of this current expose of antisemitism on the Left. Anti-Israel demonisation, some politicians think, will get those votes. The belief that, by appealing to the sentiments they think their Muslim voters hold they will secure themselves in power, may be the driver behind these abhorrent statements. This can only be cured by educating MPs and would-be MPs about antisemitism and the ethics of standing for election.

Regrettably, from the Left has emerged the programme of destruction of the only Jewish state, with its 6 million Jews conveniently gathered together. I am referring to the Boycott Divestment and Sanctions movement, which is discriminatory against Israeli nationals. Since 20% of Israel's population are Arabs, it turns out that boycotting Israeli universities is not only against the principles of the universality of science but also entails boycotting the many Arab students and lecturers in Israel's universities. BDS is antisemitic in effect, and based on double standards (for there is no similar movement against states with a much worse record of oppression and occupation, e.g. Russia, Syria, China) and should be condemned by the Party in so far as it goes beyond what is lawful (there are many statutes e.g. Equality Act, Protection from Harassment Act, charity law, limiting speech and action).

Regrettably the Labour party leader has shown himself unable to analyse this and take a stand against it. Mr Corbyn's very presence has opened up a channel for the expression of these deluded views. He has consorted with Hamas and Hezbollah; he defended Stephen Sizer, a vicar who blamed 9/11 on Jews; he has associated with Paul Eisen, holocaust denier, and Raed Salah, promoter of the blood libel. Hence simply stating that he is against racism is insufficient to remove the taint of these associations.

My recommendations are

1. That the definition of antisemitism set out above should be promulgated to the Labour Party members by the leader of the Party.

2. A party complaints procedure should be established

3. Complainants should be supported in making their complaints and protected from any backlash.

4. There should be an independent panel to determine accusations of antisemitism, sanctions against the offenders and the lifting of suspension.

5. There should be a public record of offenders, sanctions and their constituencies, if any.

Ruth Deech
3.6.16

Joint Submission by
Robert Fine Emeritus Professor, University of
Warwick and member of the Labour Party
since 1975
Christine Achinger Associate Professor,
University of Warwick)
have researched and published on relations
between antisemitism and racism, analyse the
damaging culture of suspicion that distorts
Labour Party responses, even at the highest
levels, to expressions of concern about
antisemitism, and they offer
recommendations for how the Party at all
levels might combat this culture of suspicion in
the future.

1. The Labour Party and the vast majority of its
members oppose antisemitism. This is to be
welcomed and provides a base for future
development. It should go without saying that
the Labour Party, as a progressive party,

should actively combat antisemitism whenever or wherever it shows its face and should do so with the same vigour it should show in combating other forms of racism and prejudice. Our experience, however, is that this is not the case. In our view there has been lack of leadership in combating antisemitism and poverty of theory in identifying and understanding antisemitism whether it arises from within or from without the Labour Party itself.

2. All too often we find unwillingness to confront the issue of antisemitism, doubt cast on the validity of concerns about antisemitism, distrust of the political motives of those who raise such concerns, and defensive reactions to their expression. The overall effect of these responses has been to foster within sections of the Labour Party, including its leading circles, a culture of suspicion in relation to concerns about antisemitism that is not equally present in relation to concerns about any other form of racism. This culture of suspicion is tied up with the Israel-Palestine conflict in the Middle East, insofar as it is premised on a dual prejudice,

65

first that the 'charge of antisemitism' is merely a way of disparaging criticism of Israel, and second that Israel is defended covertly and dishonestly because it cannot be defended openly and honestly.

3. What is urgently needed within the Labour Party is leadership on this issue. To this end we would recommend that the Labour Party a) commits itself in principle and practice to taking antisemitism as seriously as any other form of racism; b) encourages respectful and compassionate debate on concerns that Jews and non-Jews express about antisemitism; c) defends the right to freedom of expression against those who attempt to boycott or otherwise silence the voices of those who raise concerns about antisemitism; and c) campaigns actively for a peaceful and just settlement of the Palestinian-Israeli conflict that declares a policy of 'no tolerance' for anti-Arab, anti-Muslim or antisemitic forms of racism and supports antiracist movements and individuals both in Israeli and Palestinian society.

4. There is substantiated evidence that the problem of antisemitism is growing in the UK, Europe and globally. This unwelcome and worrying development makes it all the more important that the Labour Party commits itself to learning how to recognise and combat antisemitism alongside its commitment to recognising and combating other forms of racism and prejudice. There are those who portray current concerns about antisemitism in the Labour Party as invented by 'Zionists' in bad faith in order to smear the left and silence criticism of Israel. The Labour Party should clearly recognise that this refusal to engage with the problem of antisemitism is itself part of the problem and would not be considered an acceptable response to analogous concerns raised by any other group. In support of these recommendations we add the following observations.

5. Antisemitism, like all forms of racism, has its own peculiarities. One feature that distinguishes it from other forms of racism is its tendency to see the Jews as a hugely powerful world conspiracy. It is, therefore, a characteristic of antisemitism to present itself as a form of justified resistance in the name of the oppressed, even where it persecutes minorities. In responding to antisemitism, however, the core principle the Labour Party should observe, but in many cases is not observing, is that antisemitism and other forms of racism represent the same bankruptcy of humanity and that there are universal norms to be followed in combating them.

6. Antisemitism is indicative of a failure of democracy. Victims of antisemitic regimes and movements are not only Jews but also people in whose name antisemitic movements and regimes purport to speak. In Muslim-majority countries the first victims of antisemitic movements are more often than not other Muslims, especially antiracist Muslims. The Labour Party ought to oppose antisemitism in order to defend the rights of Jews and non-Jews attacked and vilified by antisemitic movements.

7. In the context of the Israel-Palestine conflict, combating antisemitism is not an

alternative to seeking justice for Palestinians but a pivotal part of the larger picture. These aims are inter-dependent. Antisemitism does no favour either to Jews or to the cause of justice for Palestinians. The Labour Party should not condone antisemitism within Hamas and Hezbollah any more than it tolerates anti-Arab racism within the right wing of Israeli society. A merely sanctimonious defence of Palestinians that leaves them in the same place it finds them is neither developmental nor challenging and offers no solidarity with Palestinian antiracists.

8. The Labour Party should not dismiss concerns over antisemitism on the spurious grounds that they restrict the freedom to be critical of Israel. Criticism of any country can be but does not have to be racist, Islamophobic, xenophobic or in other ways prejudiced. Similarly criticism of Israel can be but does not have to be antisemitic. Legitimate debate and criticism of Israeli politics and society – over its occupation of Palestinian land, the human rights abuses that flow from occupation, anti-Arab racism in the Israeli polity and civil society, discriminatory policies toward Palestinian citizens of Israel, military responses to aggression, etc. – does not remove responsibility to abstain from and repudiate antisemitic criticism of Israel.

9. The Labour Party should recognise that it is unacceptable to disparage through the use of derogatory language – like 'manufactured outrage', 'fake outrage', 'casting slurs', 'insinuating', 'dredging up', and 'smearing' – those who express concerns about antisemitism. Such abusive language would not be acceptable in relation to those who raise concerns over other forms of racism and is harmful at a number of levels: for example, it deters people from raising their concerns; it casts the claims of the Labour Party to consistent antiracism in a bad light; and it makes it more probable that antisemitism will be unrecognised and tolerated.

10. The Labour Party should resist any temptation to assume that the individuals and groups who raise concerns about antisemitism do so opportunistically and for illicit ends, such as destabilising the leadership of the party, protecting 'Israel' from critical scrutiny or merely pursuing private interests. Concerns over antisemitism and other forms of racism can of course be instrumentalised for other ends, but their misuse in particular cases does not invalidate the concerns themselves and does not mean that those who raise them are collectively guilty of misuse. The Labour Party should make it clear that it would be discriminatory to treat concerns about antisemitism differently from concerns about other forms of racism.

11. The Labour Party should not condone the tendency to dismiss concerns about antisemitism through the device of redefining what antisemitism is. It should not agree, with those who have refused to engage with the European Union Monitoring Commission Working Definition of Antisemitism on the grounds that it included in its definition antisemitic forms of 'criticism of Israel', like holding all Jews responsible for the actions of the state, or not recognising the distinction between state and civil society, or judging Israel by standards not applied to other states. The Labour Party should support cooperative efforts in Europe and the UK to define what

71

antisemitism is, keep the definition of antisemitism open to rational debate and revision in the light of circumstances, entertain the views of those who raise concerns about antisemitism, and involve a wide range of representative organisations of a pluralistically conceived Jewish community.

12. The Labour Party should not accept justifications of antisemitism based on the grounds that it contains a rational kernel of truth about the way 'the Jews' or many Jews are. Just as it is not acceptable to hold people of colour responsible for causing the racism of which they are victims, so too it is not acceptable to hold Jews responsible for causing antisemitism. If the Labour Party does not accept justification of anti-Black or anti-Arab racism because of the alleged or real misdeeds of African and Arab rulers, or Islamophobia because of the actions of groups claiming to speak in the name of Islam, so too it should not accept antisemitism because of the alleged or real misdeeds of the Israeli government.

13. The Labour Party has a good record of Holocaust commemoration and education, but in some quarters it is regularly maintained that memory of the Holocaust is being 'used' to legitimate the actions of the Israeli government. Memory of the historical suffering of any people can be 'used' for particular ideological ends but this is not a reason to withdraw compassion from the victims, or blot out a crucial part of the history of European barbarism, or dismiss present-day fears that the genocidal impulse toward Jews remains intact. The Labour Party should recognise that it would be discriminatory to treat Holocaust memory as peculiarly manufactured and self-serving, or as the paradigm case of victims becoming victimisers, or as the sign under which a victimised people claims ethical immunity for all its own misdeeds.

14. It would be discriminatory to impose on Jewish organisations in the Labour Party a more restrictive autonomy than on other parallel organisations. If an organisation like the Jewish Labour Movement (founded in 2004 as the successor to Poale Zion founded in

73

1905) chooses to affiliate to the 'World Zionist Movement', as is currently alleged, this is its right. It does not necessarily indicate, as is being alleged in some quarters, enthusiastic support of many Israeli government actions. It may not represent those Jews who see themselves as 'antizionist', but this is a question of democracy within the movement. No single Jewish organisation could or should be expected to represent the plurality of all Jews.

15. The temptation to practice an economy of compassion that puts all compassion on the side of Palestinians and all culpability on the side of Israel is bad politics and bad history. It supposes inter alia that the genocidal antisemitism that once infused the European continent simply vanished once Nazism was defeated. The dearth within the Labour Party of intellectual, ethical and political leadership on the issue of antisemitism stems in part at least from a failure to recognise and a willingness to tolerate antisemitism among enemies of 'Israel'.

16. The Labour Party should recognise that if it is not to be discriminatory, the ethic of conviction that declares that Israel must cease to be a 'Jewish democratic' state and must become a secular state should a) be coupled with the analogous ethic of conviction in relation to 'Arab' and 'Muslim' states; and b) be compared with other states in relation to their respective record of democracy, human rights and treatment of minorities. Finally, it should be recognised that any ethic of conviction concerning what a state ought ideally to be should be tempered by an ethic of responsibility concerning the actual forces capable of bringing about this ideal – forces that may be neither secular nor democratic and that may profess antisemitic and other racist ideologies.

Eve Garrard's Submission

research fellow in philosophy, Manchester University, points out that the main effect of the hositility to Israel shown by significant parts of the Labour Party impacts not on Israel but primarily on British Jews, who are made to feel alienated, isolated and excluded by the one-sided and ferocious focus on Israel, and the use of longstanding anti-Semitic tropes to describe the Jewish State.

There are two main points which I wish to make in this submission:
(1) concerning the impact on British Jews of current behaviour and discourse with respect to Zionism among parts of the Labour Party, especially its Left wing;
(2) concerning the effect of this on the Labour Party itself.

You are, no doubt, fully aware of how widespread hostility to Israel is among parts of the Left, including parts of the Labour Party.

One of the most cogent objections to this hostility, and to the actions it tends to produce, is that it's unfairly selective – Israel is singled out for hostile mention and treatment (for example, by the Boycott, Divestment and Sanctions campaign) where other countries whose human rights violations are much worse, are ignored or sometimes even fêted. I do not think this hostility, or even campaigns such as the BDS one, are always driven by antisemitism. But in the absence of some convincing explanation of why it is (supposedly) legitimate to focus hostility largely or entirely on Israel while practising a studied silence towards other and far worse malefactors, then the possibility of antisemitism providing the required explanation must be taken seriously. And there is such an absence – the purported explanations of the singular concern with Israel generally range from the vacuous ('We have to start somewhere') to the contemptible ('It's because Jews are really one of us, and so we have a special duty to criticise their misdeeds' – this in a world in which extensively in the past, and increasingly in the present, Jews have very definitely not been

77

regarded as 'one of us'). Something rather more plausible is needed to rule out the possibility of antisemitism being the driving force behind the anti-Israel hostilities.

However unfairness, and the legitimate concern it generates, is not the only problem arising out of the feverish focus on Israel which can be found in various left-wing arenas. If we leave aside the issue of fairness, and concentrate purely on the consequences of this singular focus, on the effects it produces, other problems come into view. For a start, the main effects are not on Israel at all – the various expressions of enmity towards Israel by significant parts of Labour's left wing have not made a lot of difference to that country, except, perhaps, to strengthen the view of many of its nationals and supporters that there really does need to be a country where Jews can't be on the receiving end of discriminatory treatment just because they are Jews.

The main effects of the hostility have been, as we might expect, on Jews in this country. Most, though not all, Jews are Zionists, and most, but not all, Zionists are Jews. Zionism has been treated by parts of the Left as a vicious and sinister ideology, to be condemned and where possible eradicated, with supporters who are likewise to be condemned and excoriated. This treatment impacts most heavily on those who regard Jewish self-determination and self-defence as important matters. These people will be primarily (though I'm glad to say not exclusively) Jews. In this way, what looks like a foreign policy issue for the Labour Party is actually an issue in domestic policy too, and a serious one for a Party which says it prides itself on being anti-racist. Antisemitism is by no means the exclusive possession of the political Right; the Left also can fall prey to that oldest of prejudices, even when (and perhaps especially when) it feels at its most certain about its own moral rectitude. And the effect on Jews, particularly ones who have in the past supported Labour, is to increase their sense of isolation and alienation. The State of Israel, which many of them see as a life-raft state which allows Jews self-determination and is committed to their defence, is the object of constant hostility and denigration by important elements in one of our major political parties. It is not surprising if this has the effect of making Jews here feel less safe, less accepted, than they were, say, in the years after the Second World War.

As a consequence of this, the Jewish vote for Labour is likely to collapse, and we are already seeing this happen in certain parts of the country. Does the Labour Party really want to be a major factor in increasing the sense of isolation and insecurity already felt by a number of Jews in this country? And does the current leadership of this party really want to be known as the one which drove the Jews out of the party? Especially since the Jews are unlikely to go quietly, and there are other political forces which will be only too happy to point out the implications of this development, and who is responsible for it.

The Labour Party cannot, and should not, attempt to prevent its supporters from holding views hostile to Israel, by any means other than open argument and debate. What it can legitimately do is discourage, and if necessary prohibit, the use of words such as 'zio' as terms of contempt and condemnation, just as it wouldn't tolerate the use of terms such as 'paki' to refer to members of a particular ethnicity. More importantly, it should take action where obviously anti-Semitic tropes such as the blood libel, or references to sinister powers pulling strings in the shadows, are being used, just as it would take action should its members, and particularly its various functionaries, refer to people of colour in terms of long-standing racist tropes against them. The Party should not be ready to regard Jews who complain about antisemitism as being dishonest and deceitful, as playing the antisemitism card; and it should actively discourage its members and supporters from doing this. It should be prepared to take decisive action where direct lies, such as the claim that Jews were the chief financiers of the African slave trade, or the claim Hitler was a supporter of Zionism, or the claim that Israel is committing genocide against the Palestinians, are promulgated. A brief suspension from the Party, followed by a silent re-admission, of people who peddle these lies does not really count as decisive action.

In the absence of such measures, which in fact would be only the first steps towards a genuine intolerance of antisemitism in the Party, Labour will be one of the factors in the production of a rising tide of hostility towards Jews in this country. And it will be peculiarly culpable for this state of affairs, precisely because it has always presented itself as hostile to all forms of racism. At the moment it is not; it tolerates, and in some cases encourages, the resurgence of an anti-semitism which some of us thought would never again be permitted the oxygen of acceptance on the Left. We were wrong, of course.

A personal note: I have voted Labour all my life. As things currently stand, I will not be able to do so again.

Eve Garrard
June 2016

Richard Gold's Submission
Member Bury South CLP

1. There have been many instances of antisemitism in the Labour Party over the years. People have complained about them, people have warned about them but nothing has ever been done until recently. People who have dared to raise the issue of antisemitism in the Party have been accused of being apologists for the Israeli government who are intent on closing down criticism of Israel. Alternatively it has been claimed that examples of antisemitism are really few and far between, and hence there is no need for any kind of action. While these antisemitic episodes have taken place within the discourse of the Palestine / Israel conflict, they have seldom actually been criticisms of Israel in themselves. They have included anti-Semitic tropes such as the idea of Jewish control, the "Zionist" lobby and dual loyalties. Some of the most obvious past examples are as listed below – it's a striking fact that none of them are criticisms of Israel or Israeli government policy. (The 2010 comments by Kaufman and

83

Linton were made at a Labour Friends of Palestine meeting.) Hopefully the current incidents of antisemitism in the current Labour Party will be acted upon in a more effective way than these examples were at the time. The more they are ignored or ineffectually dealt with by the leadership, the more they will multiply.

Tam Dalyell:
2003: In an interview in Vanity Fair, Dalyell said with reference to Tony Blair that he was unduly influenced by a "cabal of Jewish advisers".

Paul Flynn:
2011: After Matthew Gould, who is Jewish, became the British Ambassador to Israel Flynn told Sir Gus O'Donnell that the post of ambassador to Israel should go to "someone with roots in the UK".

Gerald Kaufman :
2010 "Just as Lord Ashcroft owns most of the Conservative Party, right-wing Jewish millionaires own the rest."
2011 When his Labour colleague Louise Ellman

got up to speak in the Commons he said "here we are, the Jews again",

Martin Linton :
2010 "There are long tentacles of Israel in this country who are funding election campaigns and putting money into the British political system for their own ends."

2. So there's always been antisemitism in the Labour Party. Some people say that this is not a big deal, the incidence of genuine antisemitism in the Party is very low; and suggestion that it's serious is actually a conspiracy by the right wing press and the "Israeli Lobby" to bring about the downfall of Jeremy Corbyn, with his well-known support for Palestinians. Examples of this kind of response are listed below.

Len McCluskey :
"This is nothing more than a cynical attempt to manipulate anti-Semitism for political aims because this is all about constantly challenging Jeremy Corbyn's leadership."
Jewish Socialist Group:
"Accusations of antisemitism are currently

being weaponised to attack the Jeremy Corbyn-led Labour party with claims that Labour has a "problem" of antisemitism. This is despite Corbyn's longstanding record of actively opposing fascism and all forms of racism, and being a firm supporter of the rights of refugees and of human rights globally."

Michael White

"Will someone point out to the idiots that the latest anti- Semitism row was launched by Tory blogger, Guido Fawkes & promoted by Mail on Sunday"

Jeremy Corbyn

After his brother tweeted "#Zionists can't cope with anyone supporting rights for #Palestine", (with regard to Louise Elman's comments about antisemitism in the Labour Party) Jeremy Corbyn when asked if he thought his brother's tweet was wrong went on to agree with his brother saying: "No my brother isn't wrong. My brother has his point of view, I have mine. We actually fundamentally agree – we are a family that has been fighting racism from the day we were born. My mother was at Cable Street."

This kind of response to worries about antisemitism amounts to an accusation that people who raise such worries do so purely in order to silence others, and so the charges they make are false, they are deliberately manufacturing them. This response is deeply insulting to the vast majority of Jews in the UK.

3. The current wave of antisemitic comments take place within the discourse of the Palestine / Israel debate but the criticisms are not in fact criticisms of Israel or Israeli government policy. Nobody can seriously believe that the following quotations are really criticisms of Israel.

Khadim Hussain, a Labour councillor and a former Lord Mayor of Bradford : "Your school education system only tells you about Anne Frank and the six million Zionists that were killed by Hitler."

Vicki Kirby, a Labour Parliamentary candidate tweeted that "Jews have big noses" and also asked why Isis was not attacking the real oppressor, Israel.

Gerry Downing, previously expelled from the Labour Party and then re-admitted, talked about his belief that there is a "Jewish Question" which needs to be discussed. "Why Marxists must address the Jewish Question concretely today", his publication talks about "the world 'Jewish-Zionist bourgeoisie'

Jacqueline Walker: Walker is a Vice Chair of Momentum and talked about many Jews being the chief financiers of the sugar trade and the slave trade.

4. The suspensions of several councillors, the suspension of an NEC member, the suspension of activists show that this problem is now a serious one. It can no longer be argued that it is just a few mistaken people. Many of those suspended carried a lot of influence – in their local parties, in their particular factions. While there are many supporters of the Labour Party there are not as many activists (ask anybody trying to get volunteers to do leaflet runs or supporters out during the last local elections), so activists are important and influential people.

5. The most worrying thing for the Jewish community, and there is a very large consensus over this, is that the problem of antisemitism in the Labour Party cannot be solved unless it tackles the problem with Jeremy Corbyn's views. The Jewish community to a very large extent believes that Jeremy Corbyn is a supporter of Hamas, is happy to campaign and give support to antisemites, supports the boycott of Israel and does not believe that there is actually a serious problem with antisemitism in the party. Corbyn claims not to be a supporter of Hamas, he claims to not be a supporter of antisemites, he claims that he only referred to Hamas as friends in order to be diplomatic and that he simply wants to bring the two sides of the conflict together. The Jewish community to a large extent simply doesn't believe this, and based on what he says I think their refusal to believe Corbyn's defence is correct. Corbyn has said that he doesn't believe that Hamas should be labelled as terrorists by the UK government and he believes that they are a force for good. He has said it is an honour to host Hamas and Hezbollah. With regard to Raed Saleh, the antisemite who believes that Jews use Christian blood to make bread, Corbyn has described him as someone who must be heard and that he looks forward to giving him tea on the terrace of the Commons because he deserves it.

In order for this enquiry to have any effect it needs to press Corbyn on the above. Corbyn has shown no remorse, he has never apologised for supporting people who want to kill Jews (not just Israeli Jews). Corbyn is a role model for many of the new members and supporters of the Labour Party. His influence is massive and so far his reaction to the problem of antisemitism in the party has been very poor. He has said that it isn't a serious problem, he's said that there are mechanisms in place and when it occurs it will be dealt with (he seems to think that because his family marched against Mosley he has no responsibility for what is happening in the party which he leads 70 years or more later. Compare this to John McDonnell who has said that people guilty of antisemitism in the Labour Party should be banned for life. Compare it to Tom Watson who has said that he is ashamed about antisemitism in the party and that "he would "fight to ensure that Britain's Jews always feel safe as a key part of this country and my party. I will fight to ensure that Zionism is not used as a term of abuse. Or as a code word for Jews. I will fight to ensure that the right to Jewish national self-determination is preserved and respected."

6. It's good to criticise Israel and its government when it gets things wrong, in the same way that it's good to criticise any country for its misdeeds. But it isn't good to single Israel out, it isn't good to demonise it, it's wrong to run a boycott campaign which while doing nothing for Palestinians is a campaign against a 2-states solution. This is what the Palestine Solidairty Campaign does, it's what the boycott movement does. The Labour Party needs to show commitment to a real 2-states settlement. This is an anathema to the boycott campaign and anti-Zionists in the Party. Israel is seen by them as evil, supporters of Zionism (a Jewish national state with self-determination) are seen as supporting evil (you can be a Zionist without supporting any Israeli government). This results in the demonization of the Jewish community rather than legitimate criticism of Israeli government policy. This leads to antisemitic comments even when there is no conscious antisemitic intent. It's important to realise that people don't have to be antisemitic – that is, to have antisemitic feelings – to make antisemitic comments. If the comments unfairly discriminate against Jews, then they amount to antisemitic behaviour, whatever the intentions or feelings of the commenter are. Too often the boycott campaign and anti-Zionism slip into conventional antisemitic tropes, and this means an attack on what most Jews believe.

7. I've picked up a new theme which has emerged. It's used by people who probably recognise the problem but are reluctant to admit it. It's the "I wouldn't put it like that myself but it's not antisemitic" excuse. As though being unpleasant to Jews (e.g the behaviour of the Jew-baiter Ken Livingstone) should be excused or minimised, treated merely as rudeness or bad manners, rather than racist behaviour.

8. Many previous supporters of the Labour Party in the Jewish community (some for all their adult life) now feel unable to vote Labour due to the problem of antisemitism and the track record of Jeremy Corbyn with regard to his hostility to Israel, his support for antisemites, etc. The choice is to either vote for a Party which has an antisemitism problem or to vote Tory. What a horrible choice to make – antisemitism or welfare cuts, antisemitism or benefit cuts, antisemitism or cuts in the NHS ? Support for the Labour Party in the Jewish community is at an all-time low. I myself am embarrassed to be a member of a party that is becoming more and more off bounds for the Jewish community.

9. I'm worried about the ability of this enquiry to reach a conclusion which is satisfactory to many Jewish Labour Party members and to the wider Jewish community. I hope I'm wrong but if the conclusion of the enquiry is that while there is antisemitism it's not widespread, that it's all about being civilised to each other on debates and it's about a range of legitimate views, then this enquiry will be at best ineffective. This is not about a debate between two even sides, it's a debate about antisemitism: about those who indulge in or tolerate antisemitism against the Jewish community and those who want to fight against it.

10. Writing this report is demeaning, it feels as if I have to grovel to simply play a part in getting the Labour Party to combat the problem of anti-Semitism. This shouldn't be needed, Jews shouldn't have to feel like this, in the Labour Party of 2016.

David Hirsh's Submission
Lecturer in Sociology
Goldsmiths, University of London

I have tried to keep this submission short, descriptive and clear. If the inquiry would like me to expand on anything, to clarify any points, to provide examples or evidence, then I would be happy to do so.

1. **There is antisemitism on the left**

There is nothing alien or surprising about the existence of antisemitism on the left. It has dogged our movement since the beginning. Antisemitism on the left is not only a reflection of the general prejudice that occurs throughout society, there is a specifically left wing tradition of antisemitism. It is a premise of the left that the world could be better and left wing thought seeks to find what is stopping the world from being better. Some on the left have always been tempted by the proposition that 'the Jews' stand between us and the good life; Jewish tribal selfishness is portrayed as the block to things being better for everybody. The notion that the Jews

95

prevent universal redemption has a specific Christian heritage. The notion that the Jews are at the centre of all that is wrong with the world is common to all historical antisemitisms.

The temptation to define left wing antisemitism out of existence should be resisted. Some say that the left is, by definition, opposed to antisemitism. It seems to follow that if there is antisemitism it cannot really be on the left or that if it is on the left then it cannot really be antisemitism. But taking left antisemitism seriously requires us to rely on political judgment of what is actually going on, not on definitional sophistry.

2. **There is antisemitism without conscious hatred of Jews**.

We are accustomed to the concepts of institutional and cultural racism. We are used to the idea that there can be racist ways of thinking, racist outcomes, racist norms and practices, discrimination and structural power imbalances in the absence of conscious or specifically race-motivated hatred. Racism is not only a subjective emotion inside people's heads, it is also an external and objective social phenomenon. We need to get used to the idea that antisemitism is like other racisms in this respect.

If somebody says or does something antisemitic, if they share antisemitic ways of thinking and if they participate in antisemitic norms and practices, they are not absolved from political responsibility by the fact that they feel no subjective hatred towards Jews, or that they think of themselves as opponents of antisemitism.

Antisemitism is recognized by what is said and done, not by the purity of a person's soul.

3. Bad apples or a problem with the barrel?

A bad apple theory will not do as an explanation for the current phenomenon of antisemitism on the left. We need to understand what the problem is with the barrel which has allowed so many apples to turn bad.

I do not suggest that the whole left is antisemitic or that the left is necessarily antisemitic; on the contrary, there have always been strong democratic left traditions which have understood and opposed antisemitism.

There is a relationship between a broad culture of emotional, disproportional and irrational hostility to Israel which is accepted as legitimate in much of left politics, and the specific examples of Jew-baiting by Labour people which were the catalyst for setting up this inquiry.

The examples which most people can recognise as being problematic are symptoms of the broader culture, which many people cannot recognise as being problematic. This broader culture is increasingly strong and self-confident but it is by no means uncontested.

4. **The distinction between criticism of Israel and antisemitism**

Everybody agrees that there is a distinction between criticism of Israel and antisemitism. The problem is that this truism is often interpreted such that everything is judged to be criticism and nothing is judged to be antisemitism.

Another way of articulating the principle is that there is a distinction between legitimate criticism of Israel (which we may judge to be justified or not) and demonizing or antisemitic criticism of Israel.

We are well used to judging the distinction between criticism and bigotry in other contexts. For example one may well want to make political criticisms of Hilary Clinton or Margaret Thatcher. But we know that when they are criticized for their bossiness or their masculinity, or when there is endless discussion of what they wear, or when Hilary is criticized for standing by her man, that something else is at play.

Given the long history of different antisemitisms in our culture, and specifically in left wing and radical political culture, and given the campaign to fuel an emotional anger with Israel, it would be extraordinary if antisemitic or demonizing criticism did not appear in our debates.

99

If some things are recognised as legitimate criticism and others are recognised as demonizing or antisemitic, then we are brought back into the democratic realm of rational politics. The task then is by debate and discussion to find consensus on how to draw the boundaries.

If, on the other hand, some people in practice insist that every example brought before them is legitimate criticism; while others insist that every example is antisemitic; then we remain outside the world of democratic and rational politics.

It is crucial, therefore, that the inquiry recognizes and describes why certain examples before it are not only vulgar, ignorant, rude, uncivil, but are specifically antisemitic. It must not be tempted to find cases guilty, but of a lesser charge. This would have the effect of bolstering those who insist that nothing in the antiracist movement is ever antisemitic.

Those who insist that nothing is antisemitic, that everything is just 'criticism', tend to try to

100

construct the whole problem as a battle between supporters of Israel and supporters of Palestine. They want us to take sides with the 'oppressed' in this battle and against the 'oppressors'.

Some on the edges of the trouble looking in are tempted to see it as a bad tempered and un-civil struggle, between two sets of angry 'foreigners' within our movement. This is tempting because it assigns blame in a seemingly balanced way on all sides while also absolving the poor old Brits who have to try to ensure fair play and comradely good manners. Incidentally, we see an analogous problem in judging what is criticism of Islam, what is opposition to Islamism and what is Islamophobia. Islamophobes love to declare that all they are doing is criticising Islam; Islamists enjoy portraying genuine criticism of their politics as Islamophobic.

5. **It is possible for racist discourse to be made up of legitimate elements**
Sometimes the quantity of hostility to Israel manifests itself qualitatively in easy to recognise antisemitic tropes. For example,

when people use the ostensibly antiracist vocabulary of the 'Israel lobby' to do antisemitic conspiracy theory; or when people move from concern about under-age Palestinians dying in the conflict to allegations that Israel is a child-murdering, blood-thirsty, state.

But there is a further complication. Sometimes individual claims which may be entirely legitimate on their own can swirl together into antisemitic discourse. In order to judge what is antisemitic and what is legitimate criticism it is necessary to judge the politics of a situation as a whole, taking into account the context.
If a newspaper reports street crime and rape by black men, day after day, with menacing pictures of perpetrators and bruised white innocent victims, it may well produce a racist discourse, even if every element, in itself, is not only legitimate but also true. It is not only the elements of discourse which may or may not be racist, but the way in which it all swirls together to make a whole.

For example, some might say that the analogy of Israel with apartheid South Africa is antisemitic while others might say that it is legitimate. The problem is that it could easily be either. It could be a serious and rational debate about similarities and differences; on the other hand a Jewish society on campus might be harassed, banned and isolated over a period of time as apartheid, racist and supremacist; this could constitute an antisemitic way of relating to Jewish students. The apartheid analogy is often deployed in a way which encourages people to think less rather than more, in the campaign to exclude Israelis from the global community.

6. **The construction of the 'Jewish Question'**

We have seen it said often that the claim that Labour has an antisemitism problem is invented by Zionists, Tories and Blairites to damage the Corbyn faction and the Party. Some say that there is an antisemitism problem; others respond that there is a Jewish problem; at least a problem concerning the overwhelming majority of Jews, including Labour Jews, who are defined in a hostile way as 'Zionist' or apologists for Israel.

103

There is a long history of antisemites trying to make a 'Jewish Question' part of public debate; antiracists have always responded by insisting that the 'Jewish Question' is a racist question and the real problem is a problem of antisemitism.

Is there a woman problem or a problem of sexism?
Is there a black problem or a problem of racism?
Is there a gay problem or a problem of homophobia?
Is there a Muslim problem or a problem of Islamophobia?

The conclusions of this inquiry cannot be neutral between the claim that there is a Jewish problem and the claim that there is an antisemitism problem. Between these two claims there is no room for compromise or balance.

7. The Livingstone Formulation:
A standard response to anyone who raises the issue of antisemitism on the left is the

counter-accusation that this is a bad-faith smear, mobilized to silence criticism of Israel; a playing of the antisemitism card; an attempt to mobilize Jewish victimhood to Jewish or 'Zionist' advantage.

Miners may have an interest in making the case against nuclear power but the case itself still needs to be judged on its merits.
Jews may have good reason for raising the issue of antisemitism, as black people have for raising the issue of racism and as women do for raising the issue of sexism. Indeed if people who have a long and intense memory of antisemitism racism or sexism occasionally recognise something as threatening which others may judge is not, the authentic Labour way is to relate with epathy rather than with defensive or aggressive accusations of bad faith.
Indeed people whose primary concern is to support Israel may still have good reason to raise the issue of antisemitism; they may feel that Israel was and is necessary because of antisemitism; they may feel that Israel is threatened by antisemitic movements amongst its neighbours; they may feel that the

construction of Israel as the pariah nation is analogous to the construction of the Jews as the pariah people; they may feel that talk about the decisive power of the 'Israel lobby' reflects older the older trope of Jewish power. There are four problems with the Livingstone Formulation as a response to concern about antisemitism:

a. It is a way of avoiding discussion of the actual issue of antisemitism which has been raised by deflecting attention onto the imputed motive for raising it.
b. It often functions as a form of antisemitic conspiracy theory in itself. It does not accuse Jews of being wrong – they could all be wrong independently and there is no shame in being wrong; but it accuses them of acting dishonestly, following a common, secret plan to try to help Israel in this disgraceful way.
c. It is a key mode of bullying. When a Jewish person raises the issue of antisemitism, instead of being heard respectfully, they are often themselves accused of acting dishonestly, as an agent of a foreign power, as an agent of a foreign faction or as an agent of a foreign party.

d. It trains our youth to recognise a claim of antisemitism as an indicator of Zionist dishonesty. It acts as a barrier to the education of our youth in recognising and understanding antisemitism.

The Macpherson principle does not state that somebody reporting an experience of racism is necessarily right. The principle is that it should be assumed that they could be right; that they should be listened to seriously in the process of coming to a judgment as to whether or not they are right.

The Livingstone Formulation is a clear and explicit violation of the Macpherson principle.

8. The relationship between the politics of hostility to Israel and antisemitism

The committee is faced with a formidable political problem. The problem is a profound and an established one within our broad movement and with our thinking. Solutions are far from straightforward.

There is a widespread assumption that antisemitism, when it is related to hostility to Israel, is the defensive violence of the oppressed against the oppressors. The socialism of fools, as Bebel called it, is still felt to be some form of socialism, it is felt to be something from within the family of the left. The 'Zionists', by contrast, are often situated as existing outside of the community of the oppressed and therefore outside of the community of the progressive.

Antizionism and its allied campaigns to dismantle and to boycott Israel form the intellectual and the emotional underpinnings of the culture in which antisemitic speech and actions are tolerated.

Antizionism is not simply criticism of this or that policy or characteristic or Israel. It is a political movement which takes hostility to one particular state and it makes it into an "-ism", a worldview; one which has a tendency to position the Jewish state as being central to all that is wrong with the world.
Everything bad that happens in Israel is constructed, within this ideology, as the necessary result of the supposedly racist essence of Zionism.
The aspiration to dismantle the state of Israel, against the will of its citizens, leaving them

108

defenceless against military and political forces which threaten their lives, is part of the antisemitism problem.

Politically, the analogies of Zionism with Nazism, apartheid, colonialism and racism are weaponized, not to clarify understanding but to prevent it. This encourages and licences people to relate to Jews, anyway those Jews who refuse to disavow Israel, as one would relate to Nazis, apologists for apartheid and colonialism, and racists. Relating to Jews and Jewish collectivities in this way is to relate to them in an antisemitic way.

Empirically it is demonstrable that where antizionism and the boycott campaign take hold, antisemitic discourse, exclusions and bullying follow.

A significant number of people involved in left wing and radical politics and thought in Britain today will not come close to agreeing with the description of the problem that I have offered here. That is another way of saying that there is a problem of discursive and institutional antisemitism on the British left.

Denial (the Livingstone Formulation) and expulsions (the bad apple theory) are tempting responses to the antisemitism crisis. But they will not solve the problem.

9. The democratic consensus on the issue of antisemitism

There is a clear consensus within the Jewish community on the issue of contemporary antisemitism. Jewish intellectuals, writers and leaders, as well as the institutions of the Jewish community, agree that:

a. There is a relationship between hostility to Israel and antisemitism and

b. The claim that they themselves are involved in a conspiracy to smear is part of the problem, not a helpful response to it.

There is a parallel consensus in the Jewish community in favour of a politics of peace between Israel and Palestine and a rejection of a politics of demonizing the other.

This Jewish consensus is mirrored in democratic discourse in Britain as a whole. The place where it is not mirrored in in parts of the radical left, parts of the trade union movement, amongst some intellectuals, and within parts of the Labour Party. This is an elite section of society, small, but influential. There is a small minority of Jews which strongly rejects the consensus in favour of a position which accuses the mainstream community of mobilizing an accusation of antisemitism in order to smear the left and silence those who support the Palestinians. That there are a few Jews outside of the democratic consensus should not be taken as evidence that broad consensus does not exist.

There is another wing of the Jewish community which has a keen eye for antisemitism but which slides off the democratic consensus into its own demonizing and Islamophobic understanding of Arabs and Muslims. Labour, and in particular Labour Jews, oppose this tendency.

The key institutions of the Jewish community – CST (Community Security Trust), UJS (Union of Jewish Students), BICOM (British Israel Communications and Research Centre), The Board of Deputies of British Jews, The Chief Rabbi, the leaders of all mainstream religious movements, the Jewish Leadership council, the Jewish Chronicle – are all solidly within the democratic consensus. They broadly agree on how to recognise antisemitism and they broadly agree with the perspective that Israel should aspire to find a way to end the occupation and to welcome the creation of a Palestinian state willing to live in peace with its neighbour.

10. **The antisemitism crisis is due to the mainstreaming of formerly marginal politics**
Antisemitism, as I have described it, has been a minority phenomenon on the cranky corners of the British left. Since 2001, however, it has been moving into the mainstream, and that process of mainstreaming is the cause of the current crisis.

a. Previous Labour leaders have rejected one-sided hostility to Israel and they opposed the boycott movement. They embraced the consensus of the Jewish community and of democratic politics in favour of peace, a two state solution and in rejection of the demonization of Israel and its associated antisemitism.

112

The current leader has been intentionally ambivalent on these questions. He has said he is in favour of peace and he has said he opposes antisemitism; yet he has also been hosted a number of times by Hamas in Gaza and he has articulated clear political support for Hamas; he has jumped to the defence of antisemites like Raed Salah, saying that they are victims of Zionist smears; he has acted as a figurehead for Stop the War, which has advocated war against Israel, and he has implied, for example in his response to Lord Levy, that the current antisemitism crisis is manufactured; he has been a patron of the Palestine Solidarity Campaign, which is dedicated to the politics of demonization and of boycott; he has worked for the Iranian state propaganda machine.

b. Len McCluskey, General Secretary of the biggest union in Britain, blames the crisis not on antisemitism but on a campaign to smear Labour. He is a denier.

c. Malia Bouattia, while not narrowly Labour, is now the President of the most significant youth organisation in Britain, NUS, and as such

113

she is an influential leader of the left in Britain. She openly opposes the politics of peace and she advocates that we support the politics of what she calls 'resistance'; meaning terrorism against Jewish civilians in Israel.

These three leaders are not the cause of the problem of antisemitism but they are symptomatic of its going mainstream.

11. **Antisemitism is a political problem, not one of administration**.
The key solution to the problem of antisemitism in the Labour Party is political leadership.

The party must be clear in its choice to embrace a politics of peace, reconciliation and engagement and to reject the politics of the demonization of Israel.

Israelis and Palestinians have both been caught in the global sweep of 20th and 21st Century events. Neither are villains, neither are a global players. Both nations contain people who should be Labour allies in the struggle for democracy and others of whom

114

we should be critical, and who struggle against democratic values.

The politics of peace forms a virtuous circle: it mutually reinforces democratic movements on all sides of the conflict; it takes the wind out of the sails of those who seek to mobilize hatred, racism and war.

This inquiry can and should recommend practical actions to educate the membership on the issue of antisemitism and to clamp down on people who refuse to accept the boundaries of democratic and antiracist politics. But political change is key.

If the party leadership cannot move Labour back into the mainstream democratic consensus on Israel and on antisemitism then this issue will continue to throw up crisis after crisis and it will continue to alienate most of the Jewish community; no doubt it will alienate many swing voters too.

12. Muslim antisemitism

Another space where antisemitism is over-represented the Muslim community. It should not need saying that the Muslim community is diverse and contains people of all political outlooks, including people who understand the history and the threat of antisemitism. Labour must avoid situating the problem of antisemitism as a problem of Muslims, immigrants or foreigners; equally it must avoid a racism of low expectations which fails to take Muslim antisemitism seriously and fails to require that Labour Muslims embrace democratic and antiracist politics.

There is a striking difference between the way in which Naz Shah responded to the issue of antisemitism and the way, for example, Shah Hussain responded. She apologized openly and honestly; she resolved to take steps to understand what she had done, why she had done it, and how she was going to rectify the situation. Shah Hussain, by contrast, appeared on television stony faced, denying all guilt, repeating meaningless formulations and mobilizing embarrassing counter accusations of Islamophobia.

Of course Shah Hussain must not be infantilized; he is responsible for the politics he chooses to embrace and to articulate in

116

public, in his capacity as an elected Labour councillor. But it is also true that there is a wider, non-Muslim, left-wing, scholarly and even Jewish political culture which offers sophisticated underpinnings for his attitude. The left needs to learn the lessons taught most explicitly by the experience of 'Respect', the Trotskyïst-Islamist alliance against Israel, imperialism and democracy, which did so much to mis-educate radical young people, both Muslim and not Muslim.

Naz Shah and Sadiq Khan both appear absolutely clear in their opposition to antisemitism and their willingness to engage seriously with the crisis. They are acting as leaders, fighting for a democratic politics, both within the Muslim and also the Labour communities.

The apparently delicate course Labour needs to navigate, both within and outside the Muslim community, can be defined in terms of democratic norms and values. Labour must recognise and oppose antisemitism; Labour must recognise and oppose Islamophobia; Labour must fight poverty and economic

117

exclusion, issues which impact Muslims in particular ways.

Labour must also fight anti-democratic Islamist politics; it should seek to create a pole of attraction for young people away from totalitarian resentments and towards constructive democratic ideas. It must defend the state against the totalitarian threat; and it must also defend Muslim secularists, socialists, women, lesbians and gays and dissenters against that threat.
And it is with the same democratic and egalitarian values that Labour, led by Muslim Labour members, can be at the forefront of opposing antisemitism within the Muslim community.

13. The FRA Working Definition of antisemitism

The Working Definition is not a machine for judging what is antisemitic and what is not, it cannot substitute for political judgment; but it is a set of guidelines which can help us make informed and careful political judgments. I would recommend its explicit adoption, not as legislation but as summary and a guide of what the relevant issues are in recognising antisemitism.

14. **Antisemitism is an indicator of a retreat from democratic and rational politics**
Antisemitism is a danger to Jews but it is also a danger to the Labour Party and to any other space in which it is tolerated.

There is a danger of Labour's antisemitism problem becoming a wider British antisemitism problem. At the moment, the presence of antisemitism in the party is a vote loser. We would worry even more if it became a vote-winner.
Antisemitism weakens our solidarity with those Palestinians who strive to build a democratic and free Palestinian state.

Having tried to be precise and analytical in this submission, I will finish with something else.
I took my mum to vote the other day in the mayoral election. She is 86 and Jewish; she left Hitler's Germany in 1938, aged eight. She considers herself British. She is not politically sophisticated but she is no fool. As she went to vote, she said to me that she hated Jeremy

119

Corbyn but that she was afraid that if Labour did badly then people would blame the Jews for making all that fuss about him.

I remember my dad telling me that when he was brought up in the East End, nobody, but nobody, in the Jewish community voted Tory.

Everybody was Labour.

This is the context in which allegations that the Jewish community is trying to hurt the left by manufacturing dishonest allegations of antisemitism are particularly painful.

Howard Jacobson's Submission
Trendy Anti-Zionists are reawakening
medieval hatred against Jews
Originally published in the Catholic Herald
June 24 2016
Man Booker Prize-winning novelist, critic and
broadcaster.

Anti-Semitism is still rife in society – some of it
carefully concealed. Catholics must help to
fight it.

A number of Catholic friends of mine recall
praying for my soul when they were children.
Not my soul in particular, but the souls of Jews
in general. No offence meant, but we would
not get to heaven unless we repented of our
perfidy and acknowledged Jesus Christ our
Lord. This was before Nostra Aetate,
promulgated by Pope Paul VI in 1965, which
stated that Jews were no longer to be thought
of as rejected by God. So I must presume that
my Catholic friends' children no longer pray
for the souls of my children.

121

There has been some theological coming and going on this matter since Nostra Aetate, but I take it that the Church's official position today as regards Jews is the one stated by Pope Francis earlier this year, insisting on the "unique and particular bond" we share "in virtue of the Jewish roots of Christianity", from which it follows that Jews and Christians must "consider themselves brothers, united in their God and a rich common spiritual patrimony". Clearly, any expression of anti-Semitism, in whatever form, contravenes the spirit of that bond.

But mischief lurks in the phrase "whatever form", because anti-Semitism is proving to be a versatile beast, and whereas once we knew it by the accusations the Church was wont to make, the anti-Semitic art and statuary, the libels, the yellow stars the Jews were made to wear, the pogroms and expulsions to which they were subjected in almost every corner of civilised Europe, today it finds more covert forms of expression, some of them so subtle that they come as a surprise to those who stand accused of them.

When Jeremy Corbyn, for example, insists he abhors anti-Semitism as he abhors every form of racism, there is no reason to disbelieve him. But we don't always know our own guilt and the very fact that anti-Semitism strikes him as but another example of racism is a measure of what he, taking him as in many ways typical of thinkers on the Left, doesn't understand. For anti-Semitism isn't regulation racism, not because Jews are a superior sort of victim, but because anti-Semitism is so intrinsic to the Western imagination, has played such a significant role in the conversations Christians have had with one another for 2,000 years, is so knotted about the conscience of the Church and most other institutions, that there is no mind, however liberated or modern, that doesn't have an ancient idea of the Jew lurking somewhere within it.

It isn't an accidental encounter, a new wave of migration, colour or appearance or belief system that inspires mistrust and terror of Jews; indeed, as the example of Spain after

123

the Inquisition, or even that of England in the reign of Elizabeth, shows, Jews themselves don't have to be present for anti-Semitism to prosper. The Jew, you might say, partly on account of "that rich common spiritual patrimony" of which Pope Francis speaks, is as much metaphor as fact, a metaphysical conceit, a way of conceiving of attributes of which mankind is at once fearful, envious and ashamed.

If this sounds as though I am saying that anti-Semitism is the guilty secret of which none of us is innocent and most of us unaware, then I have gone too far. But there is a touch of truth in this, and it is borne out by the recrudescence of anti-Semitism in our day, not only in the Muslim world, which has its own specific reasons for it, but in the very European countries from which we thought it must have been expelled forever only half a century ago. Some of this is overt, some of it more concealed. Of the latter form, the most insidious and contentious to talk about is anti-Zionism.

I am aware of the formulation that holds the charge of anti-Semitism against critics of Israel to be a species of blackmail, intended to silence all such criticism. But that is a species of blackmail of its own, designed to silence criticism of the critics, not every one of whom, obviously, is innocently motivated. Good faith is as variously shared between critics of Israel as it is among any other random group of personages. Some will be anti-Semites, some will not. When it comes to anti-Zionism, however, we can be more definite. Anti-Zionism gives a platform to views which in any other context would be deemed too immoderate to be acceptable.

Any understanding of events waits upon an understanding of their beginnings, but beginnings are arbitrary. Why start here when you could have started there? And who is to decide, in any instance, how far back we have to go? Allowing for the arbitrariness of starting anywhere, it is nonetheless imperative to know something of what Zionism meant to those who first gave voice to it – and by giving voice, I mean something more specific than the ancient longing to return to the land of their origin which Jews have expressed as part of their litany ever since they were forced to leave it.

The idea that the Jewish people have endured a long, destructive exile is not confined to Jews themselves. George Eliot sympathetically explored the theme of Zionism in her novel Daniel Deronda, published in 1876, the self-determination she envisaged for the Jews being more a matter of spiritual deliverance than political. Not that the two are easy to separate in the early history of Zionism. For some, Zionism was a liberation movement in the sense that it promised an end to the persecution – the expulsions, the forced conversions, the pogroms – from which Jews had enjoyed only brief periods of respite since the Middle Ages; for others, it was a liberation from the narrow, superstitious round of reiteration and ritual to which Judaism had been reduced in the shtetls of eastern Europe. The life Jews lived there, with so many restrictions placed on how they could be employed, where they could live and what they could possess, was unnatural and stunted. Forever strangers – tolerated at best

– they were, with a few exceptions, treated with suspicion and contempt, an easy prey to every wind of purposive loathing or idle vindictiveness that blew.

Not every Jew welcomed Zionism. There were those who feared it as another expression of the nationalism that had caused so much suffering in Europe. Speaking generally, their objections were honourable. They did not see in Zionism the workings of a rapacity peculiar to Jews; more a mistaken idealism. But it was an idealism rooted in recent history and non-controversial practicalities. Actual as well as imaginative affiliations with the Promised Land were already strong. Jews had been fleeing back to Palestine and building religious communities there for centuries. The most verdant of the Zionists were socialists and Bundists who imagined a near utopian existence in concord not only with existing Jewish groups but with the indigenous Arabs too. They would share the land. They would cultivate the desert together.

Were they naïve as well as desperate? Was there callousness in that naivety that blinded

127

them to the rights and, in some instances, even the existence of others who lived there? We can debate these questions till kingdom come. Just as we can argue how great a falling off from Zionism's original grand intentions modern Israel represents. But what we have no warrant to do is read backwards from the present state of things and impose its mistakes and disappointments on what was first envisaged.

The Holocaust was not a determinant of Zionism. Israel was viable well before Hitler. But if there were questions as to Zionism's necessity – and the alternative for many sophisticated European Jews had been a vague, impractical universalism – the Holocaust answered them. Beyond doubt now, with so many countries if not bent on their extermination then at the very least mortally hostile to them, and with so many others, deemed friendly, imposing quotas and closing their borders, Jews had nowhere but Israel to flee to. The very fears to which early Zionists had given voice were borne out by history: stateless, the Jews were doomed.

So where does this leave the person – let him be a Christian or a socialist – for whom Zionism is at its very heart a tool for supremacist colonial oppression and Israel, as a consequence, eternally illegitimate? Either he admits his ignorance of Zionism's life-and-death significance for Jews, or he declares himself in retrospect indifferent to their fate.

It matters not one bit that in his own eyes he is no anti-Semite. Few of us act in full consciousness of what sways us. That person is rare whose every thought is rigorously tested against reason and dispassion. So I say only this: to reject Zionism out of hand, to refuse Jews, alone of all peoples, the right to self-determination and therefore the right to safety, is to embrace the logic of anti-Semitism if not its conclusions. The fact that on some university campuses "Zio" has become a term of abuse hurled at Jews, performing the very function "Yid" once did, proves this incontrovertibly. Regardless of what's intended, in effect anti-Zionism is just the same old anti-Semitism in a differently labelled bottle.

Am I arguing that no criticism of Israel as a political entity can be valid? No, I am not. There is, in my view, some savage mirth to be had at the expense of those who speak of being "critical" of Israel – "critical" suggesting the employment of fine tools of demurral and discrimination, when the language they employ is inflammatory and hyperbolic, proclaiming every battle a massacre, every war a genocide, and every security provision apartheid – still and all, it is the duty of a friend, regardless of what enemies propose, to point out faults. But the distinction is crucial: wanting Israel to act other than it currently does is one thing; denying its right to be there, or calling into question the motives of its origins, is another.

This still, however, does not render all acts of censure of Israel obligatory and inviolable. It must not be required of a Jew that he denounce Israel before he is allowed a platform. Wherever disagreement is refused, bigotry is at work. The ferocity with which the anti-Israel agenda is pursued should itself gives us pause. In an unjust and barbaric world, why does the injustice of the Israeli occupation resound with such particularity for us?

I am not going to say, because it is a Jewish state. But let me ask the question: how is that in the fury of anti-Zionist dialectic and demonstration are to be found caricatures of Jews that any churchman of the Middle Ages would recognise immediately – grinning gargoyles on the great cathedrals, implacable demons, sulphurous, bloodthirsty monsters convinced of their own divine election and murderously contemptuous of other people and other faiths? It is right that Christians should speak up for the oppressed. But compassion must not be bought at the price of prejudice.

If this is truly a time to affirm the ancient spiritual bond between Christians and Jews, it cannot be a time to tolerate the ancient cartoons that made of Jews a Satanic race. See Zionism through the prism of a medieval suspicion of the Jewish character, and Israel as the working out of Zionism's diabolic intentions, and you have brought the Devil back among us

131

Owen Power's submission

MPhil, Unvester, University of Manchester, equality campaigner, member of Salford Labour Party

My submission, it is not an attempt to be scholarly, but it is from the heart.

Greetings from Salford Shami !

I am a man in my 60s, British, Jewish, gay, deaf, an immigrant, and proud!

I think the UK is a great country to live. I feel one of the factors which contributes to its greatness is the tradition of justice and fairness in the Labour Party. The Labour Party was the vanguard for equality for women, racial equality, and LGBTQ equality and I have an enormous sense of gratitude to the party for that.

However, I am very uneasy about the emerging tolerance of antisemitism, sometimes in the guise of anti-Zionism and

Israel- hatred which is becoming apparent within the Leadership of the party. It is difficult to understand why such people as Sir Gerald Kauffman and Ken Livingstone are not expelled from the party, just to give two examples. There is no need for me to repeat what others will submit.

For me, all the advantages of living in the UK come to nothing if anti-Semitism is unchecked and it is no longer safe for Jews to live here. Jews need and stand by Israel, not for lofty 'theological' or 'Imperial' ideas, but simply as a place of safety from hatred; I am sure you don't need evidence for that.

Of course criticism of this or that Israeli government policy can be valid and sometimes is, but when Israel is singled out exclusively it is Jew-hatred in a flimsy disguise.

I am happy to report I have met with my MP Rebecca Long-Bailey and she has publicly declared antisemitism has no place here in Salford. In addition, Salford City Council does great work for local people and I am confident the Council does everything to combat antisemitism within the community such as the desecration of Jewish gravestones.

I sincerely hope this inquiry results in the Labour Party Leadership having an honest review, which will go some way to restore confidence that it is still safe for Jews to live here.

With all good wishes,
Owen
Owen Power BA (Hons) MA (Jewish Studies) MPhil (University of Manchester).

Stephen Spencer Ryde's Submission
To the chair of the inquiry, Shami Chakrabarti

I am writing to you to formally submit evidence to this inquiry as a British Jew, an active member of the Jewish community and someone who has been affected deeply by the recent and still ongoing opprobrium from Party members about Jews.

My evidence starts in October 2015. I attended a Palestinian Return Centre meeting at Parliament. At this event I watched Labour's most senior MP, Sir Gerald Kaufman, publicly state that "Jews paid blood money to the British government to obfuscate and lie for the benefit of Jews in the State of Israel." This was a mendacious lie founded on a classic form of Jew hatred, that being Jews having unparalleled wealth which they used to manipulate governments and authorities to their advantage and against the greater good. Not only did this elicit howls of appreciation from the audience (inciting this racist narrative) but also was applauded by another Labour MP, Andy Slaughter, who stated that he agreed with every word. At this meeting other antisemitic stories were aired such as Jews owning the gold of Fort Knox and Israelis being child murderers and harvesting organs of children for medical use. Blood libels that I thought could never be heard in the heart of our parliament.

At this point I wrote to the Labour Party: Jeremy Corbyn, Rosie Winterton and John Mann (in his capacity as Chair of the All Party Parliamentary Group against Antisemitism). I declared that I had experienced antisemitism first hand. Labour's official response: "Sir Gerald could apologise if he wished to". He never did. Matter closed.

Since then I have written hundreds of polite emails to the Party every time antisemitic activity has reared its ugly head in the Party, whether that be MPs, councillors, activists, members, union leaders or high profile supporters.

The Party has replied twice to my emails. Despite me telling the recipients how hurt, offended and intimidated I feel at every new antisemitic revelation and despite the fact that my family are genuinely upset and in fear.

My 10 year old daughter feels ashamed of her Judaism. She is aware of Jew Hate through the media and is confused when she hears a politician talking about the Jewish State being "transported" to resolve the differences between Israel and its neighbours or "Israel being racist". She is a kid who visits her family and friends in Tel Aviv but now feels ashamed because of these vicious untruths.

My 19 year old daughter is at university. She wears an "I love Tel Aviv" tee-shirt. But she knows not to get involved in politics with some students who will intimidate her quoting "Hamas as friends". This is the same Hamas who, in their charter "demand the extermination of all Jews". She accepts that her social media is invaded with invites to PSC and BDS events where she hears antisemitic canards freely bandied around as truths and has to explain to her friends that this is not the Israel she loves.

My wife stopped watching the news because she found the continuous stream of antisemitic revelations in Labour too much to cope with. She has begun to talk about leaving the UK. She believes there is no future for Jews in the UK when a major political party can openly speak with opprobrium against Israel and Jews.

Labour voting Jewish friends have resigned their membership. I met a dear friend outside the gates of our synagogue (where I was doing my security duty, as necessary at every Jewish venue). Her mother, 80 years old and a lifelong Labour activist and ex councillor looked at me and said how sorry she was for the hatred in Labour towards Jews. She felt responsible. Wrong though that responsibility was, her grief at something she had loved all of her life turning against her and her community was heartbreaking.

I watched our Jewish representatives, The Board of Deputies, meet with Jeremy Corbyn. I know these representatives. They are decent upstanding people. Their disappointment in Jeremy's engagement was obvious.

Jeremy's intransigence towards the issue created even greater dismay for the community. It was compounded by his friendship towards Jews latest persecutors, Hamas; his friendship with a Holocaust denier; his platforming with Jewish hate speakers; his inability to say the word "Israel" in a speech to Labour friends of Israel; his continued support of anti Israel organisations such PSC and Stop the War; his reluctance to deal with antisemitism in general. Jeremy Corbyn's silence as the mainstream Labour vessel started to rock with the tidal wave of bigotry towards Jews and that which they hold precious was shocking. This was the Leader of Her Majesty's Opposition letting racism rage.

We, as Jews, have been hurt, offended and intimidated. We now live in fear. This is the sentiment of the vast majority of Jews. Not the tiny sample who are unquestioningly loyal to Labour and call antisemitism a smear campaign.

When Dianne Abbott appeared on BBC and stated that "Labour did not have an

139

antisemitism problem" despite the Chief Rabbi, the Board of Deputies, the Campaign Against Antisemitism and the Chair of the All Party Government against Antisemitism and almost all Jews saying otherwise, she implied that Jews were too stupid to know what constituted antisemitism or were simply liars. Clearly she felt that MacPherson did not apply to Jews (unlike her colleagues John MacDonnell and Baroness Royall who both were clear that this was a valid test of antisemitism as with any other form of racism). Somehow Dianne Abbott thought that hate against Jews was an exception. Whatever Jews felt before this interview, she compounded all the negative and fearful emotion that Jews were experiencing.

Almost every Jew I know, and I know thousands, from every walk of life, from every different background, of every age and every political persuasion consider the future bleak for Jews in the UK, much because of the behaviours I have just outlined. We see historical similarities and this time Jews will not wait to see how this plays out. All across

Europe Jews are fleeing to the only place they feel safe, Israel.

I met a senior representative of the Israeli government. She asked me, "Are you ok? We worry about you in Britain". She told me how Israel understands its neighbours and the feelings towards Israelis. It has many ways to defend itself and does so in a fully committed way to its people (all Israelis of course, all races and religions). But in Britain we are at whim of those who don't care so much. Being such a small minority, Jews in the UK may not to be able to defend themselves. Israelis, despite their challenges think we are truly on the front line; they think British Jews are the real ones under threat.

Labour can address this. Labour can once again be the best friends to Jews, Israelis and Zionists. We are the most natural of bed fellows. Our histories of equality, industry and social inspiration should make us the proudest of friends. Our battles against racist bigotry put us on the same path. Cable Street was the Socialists and the Jews.

On the 30th May 2016 the International Holocaust Remembrance Alliance, the world's most authoritative organisation on antisemitism agreed to formally adopt the Working Definition of antisemitism. Here is the press release:

The International Holocaust Remembrance Alliance (IHRA) adopts a working definition of antisemitism on 26 May.

The consensus decision on the adopted decision was reached after in-depth discussion of the issue during the IHRA Plenary meetings held in Bucharest from 23-26 May.

IHRA chair, Ambassador Mihnea Constantinescu, stated:

"All IHRA Member Countries share concern that incidents of antisemitism are steadily rising and agree that IHRA's Member Countries and indeed IHRA's experts need political tools with which to fight this scourge. IHRA's 31 member countries- 24 of which are EU member countries- are committed to the Stockholm Decision and thereby to fighting

142

the evil of antisemitism through coordinated international political action."

The IHRA Chair continued: "By adopting this working definition, the IHRA is setting an example of responsible conduct for other international fora and hopes to inspire them also to take action on a legally binding working definition."

The Chair underlined the fact that as a body of 31 member countries, ten observer countries , and seven international partner organisations with a unique mandate to focus on education, research and remembrance of the Holocaust, the IHRA was the appropriate body to adopt a working definition of antisemitism. The IHRA Chair noted the fundamental role that the German OSCE Chairmanship-in-Office played in facilitating the adoption of the working definition.

Mark Weitzman, Chair of the IHRA Committee on Antisemitism and Holocaust Denial, which proposed the adoption of the definition in 2015, said: "In order to begin to address the problem of antisemitism, there must be clarity

143

about what antisemitism actually is. This is not a simple question. The adopted working definition helps provide guidance in answer to this challenging question. Crucially, the definition adopted by the IHRA is endorsed by experts, is relevant and is of practical applicability. Together with the IHRA adopted Working definition of Holocaust Denial and Distortion, the working definition of antisemitism provides another tool in the IHRA tool kit for combatting antisemitism."

This inquiry must adopt the same definition. This is it in full:

Bucharest, 26 May 2016

In the spirit of the Stockholm Declaration that states: "With humanity still scarred by ...antisemitism and xenophobia the international community shares a solemn responsibility to fight those evils" the committee on Antisemitism and Holocaust Denial called the IHRA Plenary in Budapest 2015 to adopt the following working definition of antisemitism.

On 26 May 2016, the Plenary in Bucharest decided:

To guide IHRA in its work, the following examples may serve as illustrations:

Manifestations might include the targeting of the state of Israel, conceived as a Jewish collectivity. However, criticism of Israel similar to that levelled against any other country cannot be regarded as antisemitic. Antisemitism frequently charges Jews with conspiring to harm humanity, and it is often used to blame Jews for "why things go wrong." It is expressed in speech, writing, visual forms and action, and employs sinister stereotypes and negative character traits.

Contemporary examples of antisemitism in public life, the media, schools, the workplace, and in the religious sphere could, taking into account the overall context, include, but are not limited to:

Calling for, aiding, or justifying the killing or harming of Jews in the name of a radical ideology or an extremist view of religion.

145

Making mendacious, dehumanizing, demonizing or stereotypical allegations about Jews as such or the power of Jews as collective – such as, especially but not exclusively, the myth about the world Jewish conspiracy or of Jews controlling the media, economy, government or other societal institutions.

Accusing Jews as a people of being responsible for real or imagined wrong doing committed by a single Jewish person or group, or even for acts committed by non-Jews.

Denying the fact, scope, mechanisms (e.g. gas chambers) or intentionality of the genocide of the Jewish people at the hands of National Socialist Germany and its supporters and accomplices during World War II (the Holocaust).

Adopt the following non-legally binding working definition of antisemitism:

"Antisemitism is a certain perception of Jews, which may be expressed as hatred toward Jews. Rhetorical and physical manifestations of antisemitism are directed toward Jewish or non-Jewish individuals and/or their property, toward Jewish community institutions and religious facilities."

Accusing the Jews as a people, or Israel as a state, of inventing or exaggerating the Holocaust.

Accusing Jewish citizens of being more loyal to Israel or to the alleged priorities of Jews worldwide, than to the interests of their own nations.

Denying the Jewish people their right to self-determination, e.g., by claiming that the existence of a State of Israel is a racist endeavour.

Applying double standards by requiring of it a behaviour not expected or demanded of any other democratic nation.

Using the symbols and images associated with classic antisemitism (e.g., claims of Jews killing Jesus or blood libel) to characterize Israel or Israelis.

147

Drawing comparisons of conemporary Israeli policy to that of Nazis.

Holding Jews collectively responsible for actions of the state of Israel.

Antisemitic acts are criminal when they are so defined by law (for example, denial of the Holocaust or distribution of antisemitic materials in some countries).

Criminal acts are antisemitic when the targets of attacks, whether they are people or property – such as buildings, schools, places of worship and cemeteries – are selected because they are, or are perceived to be, Jewish or linked to Jews.

Antisemitic discrimination is the denial to Jews of opportunities or services available to others and is illegal in many countries.

Finally, I implore this inquiry to hold true to this definition, hold true to its values and that of a decent political party where these criminal antisemitic acts and behaviours are banished along with all those who hold these despicable views. They have no place in the Labour Party. They never did and they never will do. Make me, my family, my friends and my community feel that Jews are welcomed by, not hated by the Labour Party.

SINCERELY

STEPHEN SPENCER RYDE

Noru Tsalic MBA,
Management Consultant and Political
Commentator

Dear Ms. Chakrabarti,
In relation to the inquiry into antisemitism in
the Labour Party, I would like to submit the
following:

I am a member of the Jewish community and a
former member of the Executive Committee
for the Coventry Reform Jewish Community. I
am not a member of any political party – my
vote is driven by what I consider each time to
be in the best interest of the nation, rather
than by any ideological inclination.

I cannot speak for the entire British Jewish
community – that is the job of the Board of
Deputies. However, all the Jews I personally
know have been greatly offended and worried
by the anti-Semitic outbursts that came – of all
places! – from the ranks of the Labour Party, a
political party that claims to be fundamentally
anti-racist. The issue has become a subject of
constant concern in our homes, around the
dinner table and in our communities. There is

150

also a sense of betrayal among many Jews who have always seen themselves as Labour voters and supporters.

The opinions below are my own, but they have crystallised through many a discussion I had with fellow Jews. To better understand the issues, I have also read submissions to the inquiry from other quarters. (e.g. [1])

Jews, Judaism, Jewishness
I apologise if the concepts below are obvious to you, but I do believe that they are complex and need to be defined from the perspective of the Jews themselves. I think you will find that the vast majority (though by no means all!) of Jews in this country will agree with these definitions.

While Judaism is a monotheistic religion like Islam and Christianity, Jews are not 'a religion'. We are a people, i.e. an ethno-religious and cultural community bound together by a sense of common identity and solidarity.

151

Although in principle converts to Judaism are considered Jews, such conversions are rare. Judaism is not a proselytising religion; the vast majority of Jews have acquired that identity through birth, rather than through conversion. People can simultaneously have multiple identities and Jewishness is one of the identities that British Jews hold. One can be a Jew, a British national, a socialist, a vegan, a believer in animal rights, etc. Many people of Jewish descent manifest a very strong sense of Jewish identity; for others it is weak or almost nonexistent in comparison to their other identities.

Clearly, it is not sufficient to be 'of Jewish descent' to be a Jew from the point of view of the sense of identity. However, it is difficult to precisely define at which point a person of Jewish descent should no longer be considered 'a Jew'. Most Jews would consider a person of Jewish descent to be a Jew if s/he maintains some level of religious and cultural affiliation, even if s/he does not believe in God and/or does not strictly observe the precepts of Judaism. There is a small number of ritual items that the vast majority of Jews (whether religious or not) perform at set times in their lives and consider essential to their identity: circumcision of male children, bar-mitzvah (the religious rite of passage to maturity), wedding, burial. Most Jews also celebrate Jewish festivals (especially the Jewish New Year and Passover) and mark the Day of Atonement. Most British Jews would consider a person of Jewish descent who does not perform those minimal items as 'alienated' or 'estranged' from his/her Jewish identity. The vast majority of Jews see conversion to another religion as the definite loss of a person's Jewish identity.

Israel

The term 'Jew' was initially an exonym derived from the Greek Ἰουδαῖος, through the Latin Judaeus (meaning Judean, or inhabitant of Judea). 'Israel' was the endonym for 'the Jewish people'. The Old Testament, for instance, refers to Jews as בני ישראל (B'nei Israel, Children of Israel), עם ישראל ('Am Israel, People of Israel), or simply ישראל (Israel, see for instance 2 Samuel 7:23-24). In the Qur'an,

153

Jews are called بَنُو اِسرَائيل (Banū Isrā'īl, the Children of Israel).

The Jewish homeland was traditionally called 'Eretz Israel' (The Land of Israel) and it is from there that the name of the modern state comes, in the same way in which Finland means 'Land of the Finns'.

The vast majority of British Jews (as evidenced by several opinion polls, see for instance [2]) view Israel as central to their Jewish identity. Strong connection with a different place/country is not unique to Jews, it exists among other minority ethnic communities in Britain. [3]

However, in the case of Jews the connection is most likely stronger, for two reasons:

1.   A religious reason: the centrality of the Land of Israel in Judaism;

Judaism never attained the status of 'global religion', but remained an ethnic or 'tribal' faith. This implies a stronger geographic element. In Judaism, the Land of Israel (also called Eretz HaKodesh – the Holy Land) acquired a sacred character, which was bequeathed to a certain extent to both Christianity and Islam. Jerusalem ('Ir HaKodesh, the Holy City) is seen as the sacred

154

centre of the Holy Land; the Temple Mount (which became identified with Mount Zion) is seen as the epicentre of holiness, the half-celestial-half-earthly residence of the Divine Presence. Wherever they are, Jews pray facing towards Jerusalem. The importance of the Land of Israel and of Jerusalem suffuses Judaic scriptures and ritual.

2.   A national reason: 2,000 years of statelessness;

One of the main reasons states exist is to provide their citizens with security. As an exiled, stateless people persecuted through much of their history, Jews were particularly in need of such security. From our point of view, statelessness came at a horrific price, culminating with the lack of protection and refuge during the Holocaust. Throughout history, the Jew's status of perennial 'refugee' (the 'Wandering Jew') has generated contempt and has reinforced antisemitic sentiment among 'host peoples'.

Zionism

Most definitions of Zionism (see for instance [4]) call it "a political movement" or "an ideology" and mention that it "emerged

155

towards the end of the 19th century". Most such definitions add attributes like "European", "Jewish", "nationalist" and "secular". Many mention that it emerged "as a result of antisemitism".

Such definitions are reductionist in the extreme. They usually serve anti-Zionist political aims: if Zionism is "European", "Jewish", "nationalist" and "secular"; if it "emerged at the end of the 19th century", then it follows that it has nothing to do with the Middle East, with Judaism or with ancestral aspirations.

But the Chief Rabbi of Britain, Rabbi Ephraim Mirvis appears to contradict that thesis. Recently, he called Zionism [5]

"a noble and integral part of Judaism. Zionism is a belief in the right to Jewish self-determination in a land that has been at the centre of the Jewish world for more than 3,000 years. One can no more separate it from Judaism than separate the City of London from Great Britain."

Rabbi Mirvis is supposed to know a thing or two about Judaism. But he does not require his opinion to be taken on faith; rather, he goes on to write:

"Open a Jewish daily prayer book used in any part of the world and Zionism will leap out at you. The innumerable references to the land of Israel are inescapable and demonstrative." Judaism's main prayer book is called the Siddur. Amidah is arguably Siddur's centre-piece prayer – it is recited (standing up, rather than sitting) as part of every synagogue service. It includes the following supplication (translation from Hebrew):

"Sound the great Shofar [an ancient trumpet-like instrument made from the horn of a ram] *for our freedom; raise a banner to gather our Diasporas, and bring us swiftly together from the four corners of the Earth into our Land. Blessed are You Lord, Who gathers the exiles of His people Israel."*

Amidah was not concocted (by either mythical "Elders of Zion" or real-life Zionists) in the 19th century. It dates from around the 2nd century CE. Observant Jews everywhere have been reciting it three times a day ever since. Less observant Jews like myself – whenever we happen to attend a synagogue service.

Passover's ritual Seder meal (one of those basic traditions that most non-observant Jews

157

also perform) ends with the wish *"Next year in Jerusalem"*. Again, this is a tradition that has been around for many hundreds of years. Rabbi Mirvis went on to state:

"Throughout our collective history we have yearned for a chance to determine our own future, to revive an ancient language and return to rejoice in our love for this tiny sliver of land."

For lack of space or of journalistic interest, his article did not explain that statement. I take the liberty to do so, by listing here a selection of historical events which preceded the 19th century:

66–73 CE: 'Great Jewish Revolt' against Roman occupation. After defeating it, the Romans demolish the Temple. Jews are prohibited from entering Jerusalem and are gradually expelled from the Land of Israel.

115–117:   'Rebellion of the Exile'. Exiled Jews in several corners of the Roman Empire rise against the Romans and return to the Land of Israel. They are eventually defeated.

132–135:   'Bar Kokhba revolt'. Jews rise against the Romans under the leadership of Bar Kokhba. They regain Jerusalem, proclaim independence, even make coins with the text 'To the freedom of Jerusalem'. They are ultimately defeated by superior Roman forces. Emperor Hadrian prohibits the practice of Judaism. He prohibits the terms 'Israel' and 'Judaea' and re-names the country 'Syria-Palaestina' after the Philistines, the ancient enemies of the Jews.

351–352: 'Revolt against Gallus'. Jewish revolt liberates Galilee, before being defeated.

362-572: Several Samaritan revolts against Byzantine rule. The Samaritan faith (a sect of Judaism which had survived in the Judean Hills) is outlawed.

602-628: Persian Jews form an army, join forces with the Sassanids against the Byzantines and reconquer Jerusalem. A semi-autonomous Jewish state is declared, but is ultimately defeated in 628.

636: Arab conquest of 'Syria' (including the Land of Israel). Jews are initially allowed back into Jerusalem, but are later prohibited again from entering. The Al Aqsa Mosque and the Dome of the Rock are built on the site of the destroyed Jewish Temple.

1160:   Revolt of Jews in Kurdistan.
Failed attempt to reconquer the Land of Israel.
1198:   Jews from Maghreb arrive
and settle in Jerusalem.
1204:   Moshe Ben Maimon
(Maimonides) dies and is buried in Tiberias, on
the shores of the Sea of Galilee.
1211:   Around 300 Jews from
England and France manage to reach the Land
of Israel and settle in Jerusalem. The majority
are killed by the Crusaders in 1219. The few
remaining are exiled from Jerusalem and find
refuge in Acre.
1217:   Judah al-Harizi (rabbi,
translator, poet and traveller who travelled
from Spain to the Land of Israel) bemoans in
his writings the state of the Temple Mount.
1260:   Having settled in the Land of
Israel, Yechiel of Paris (French rabbi)
establishes a Talmudic academy in Acre.
1266:   Jews banned from entering
the Cave of the Patriarchs in Hebron.
1267:   Nachmanides (leading
medieval Jewish scholar from Catalonia)
arrives in Jerusalem; Ramban synagogue
established.

1286:   Meir of Rothenburg (famous
rabbi and poet from Germany) is incarcerated
after attempting to emigrate to the Land of
Israel.

1355:   Physician and geographer
Ishtori Haparchi (born in France and settled in
the Land of Israel) dies in Bet She'an.

1428:   Jews attempt to purchase
the Tomb of David; the Pope issues a
prohibition for ship captains to carry Jews to
the Land of Israel.

1434:   Elijah of Ferrara (famous
Talmudist and traveller) settles in Jerusalem.

1441:   Famine forces Jerusalem's
Jews to send emissaries to European Jews,
asking for help.

1455:   Failed large scale
immigration attempt starting from Sicily. The
would-be immigrants are condemned to
death, but the punishment is commuted to a
heavy fine.

1474:   Great Synagogue of
Jerusalem demolished by Arab mob.

1488:   Obadiah ben Abraham of
Bertinoro arrives in Jerusalem on March 25,
1488, having commenced his journey October
29, 1486. When, following the expulsion of

the Jews from Spain in 1492, many of the exiles settled in Jerusalem, Bertinoro became their intellectual leader. These Spanish Jews presented Bertinoro with a site for a yeshivah (religious academy) in Jerusalem, which he founded. Considerable support for the maintenance of the yeshivah was given by the Jews of Egypt and Turkey at Bertinoro's written solicitation.

1493:   Joseph Saragossi travels from Spain and settles in Safed. He becomes the leader of the local Jewish community and dies in 1507.

1561:   Spanish Jews travel to the Land of Israel under the leadership of Don Joseph Nasi. They settle in Safed. Joseph Nasi secures permission from Sultan Selim II to acquire Tiberias and seven surrounding villages to create a Jewish city-state. He hoped that large numbers of Jewish refugees and Marranos (Jews forced to convert to Catholicism) would settle there, free from fear and oppression; indeed, the persecuted Jews of Cori, Italy, numbering about 200 souls, decided to emigrate to Tiberias. Nasi had the walls of the town rebuilt by 1564 and attempted to turn it into a self-sufficient textile manufacturing centre by planting mulberry trees and producing silk. Nevertheless, a number of factors during the following years contributed to the plan's ultimate failure. But by 1576, the Jewish community of Safed faced an expulsion order: 1,000 prosperous families were to be deported to Cyprus, 'for the good of the said island', with another 500 the following year. The order was issued as an instrument of extortion: it was rescinded once a hefty bribe was extracted from the Jews in the form of 'rent'.

1648:   Jews from Turkey attempt to return as a group to Israel, under the leadership of Sabbatai Zevi. His arrival in Jerusalem triggers an anti-Jewish pogrom.

1700:   A group of 1,500 Ashkenazi Jews attempt to travel to the Land of Israel under the leadership of Rabbi Yehuda he-Hasid. A third die on the way. The Rabbi himself dies within days of arrival. The survivors settle in Jerusalem.

1764-1850:   Small groups of Jews (between 5 and 500 each) make their way to the Land of Israel under various rabbis.

It's not, then, that Zionism was "a 19th century political movement". It is that it became a political movement in the 19th century – acquiring in the process its modern name and 'ism' suffix. The aspiration (or rather the craving) was there in every previous century – or in every generation; it's just that it took such extent and form that suited the times. One can hardly expect any "political movement" – let alone a Jewish one – to have appeared as such in the 15th century. In fact, in the 15th century Zionism was so much an integral part of Judaism that people who believed in it (and put it in practice whenever possible) thought they were only practicing their religion.

No wonder, then, that Rabbi Mirvis concluded: *"to those people who have nevertheless sought to redefine Zionism, who vilify and delegitimize it, I say: Be under no illusions – you are deeply insulting not only the Jewish community but countless others who instinctively reject the politics of distortion and demonisation."*
Britain's previous Chief Rabbi, Lord Sacks, agrees [6]:

164

"Anti-Zionism is the new anti-Semitism."

Anti-Semitism

The vast majority of British Jews will agree that antisemitism is racism directed against Jews. Despite its name (a misnomer invented by an anti-Semite), it has nothing to do with 'Semites' or 'Semitic people' ('Semitic' really applies to a family of languages, not a 'race' or to a group of people). Antisemites hold racist views about Jews, but not necessarily about Arabs and Ethiopians (who also speak Semitic languages).

Like all racism, antisemitism can take many forms – from subliminal prejudice and stereotypes to violent attacks and everything in-between. People can hold racist views without necessarily expressing them. One can hold a prejudice (and be driven by it) without consciously admitting it. One can even actively support anti-racist causes, while harbouring racist views. The incidence of racist views among white abolitionists in the US, for instance, is well-known and often analysed in the literature.

165

Since racist prejudice can be subliminal, how can society recognise manifestations of racism? Typically, it is easy to recognise such manifestations in historical retrospect, once the society has 'made up its mind' about it. For instance, use of the word "nigger" is recognised nowadays as racist. But only a few decades ago, one could use the word while considering oneself 'a good person' and even an anti-racist [7]. The reason that the word came to be recognised as racist is that most African Americans find it offensive.

The point of all this is that what constitutes a manifestation of racism is best defined by the victimised community, the one that experienced racism and is most sensitive to its manifestations. It is not up to white people to judge what black people should or should not find offensive. And it is not up to non-Jews to define what Jews should or should not perceive as antisemitic.

'Good Jews' and 'Bad Jews'
People accused of antisemitism often point out that their views are supported by/based on opinions of some Jews (sometimes even

Israeli Jews) – the implication being that they cannot possibly be antisemitic.

This is a strident fallacy.

Firstly, as explained before, not everybody who is "of Jewish descent" or has a recognisable Jewish name should automatically be considered a Jew. US President Barack Obama has a Swahili first name, a Muslim middle name and is of Kenyan descent. Yet he is American (not just by citizenship, but in terms of his sense of identity) and cannot speak on behalf of Swahili-speaking Africans, Muslims or Kenyans.

British-Jewish author Howard Jacobson has famously coined the term "As-a-Jew" [8] to describe people of Jewish descent who preface criticism of Jews, Israel or Zionism with the words "As a Jew…" – in an attempt to impart additional 'weight' to that criticism.

167

For some of "As-a-Jews", that criticism is the

only manifestation of their "Jewishness."

Secondly, like any other community, Jews hold a wide range of opinions. It is unclear why some people seem to implicitly request that **all** Jews (rather than **most** Jews) should agree with a certain view, before it is taken to represent the collective view of the community. Such standard of "unanimity" is not required of any other community. By such standard, use of the n-word should not be viewed as racist (despite being offensive to most black people), if a small minority of black people supports that use.

In fact, most Jews find arguments like "Not all Jews are Zionists" and "Before WWII, most Jews were not Zionists" as themselves inappropriate and expressing a prejudice. Why would "all Jews" be anything – one does not expect "all Muslims" or "all Swedes" to agree on anything? How is what past generations of Jews believed (assuming one knows what most of them believed),relevant

168

to how most Jews feel today? Should we sanitise the n-word because past generations of African Americans might not have considered that word offensive? Before WWI, the notion of independence from the Ottoman Empire might have been supported only by a minority of Arab people. Is that relevant to how Arabs feel about independence today?

In the case of other groups of people (including the Labour Party), it is accepted practice that their "collective view" is expressed by their elected representatives – even though, of course, minority opinions exist within the group. It is unclear, therefore, why the views of the Board of Deputies (the elected representatives of the British Jewish community) are ignored. How come that the Board is not represented on a panel investigating anti-Jewish views and activity in the Labour Party?

Thirdly, some Jews (or "people of Jewish descent") can themselves harbour antisemitic prejudice, make antisemitic comments and even commit antisemitic acts. This is no different than in the case of any other

169

community or group of people. Before the abolition of slavery in USA, some freed black people have themselves been slave-owners. Even nowadays, a few African Americans can be heard disparaging their own community. That, surely, constitutes no excuse for slavery, nor does it justify anti-black prejudice.

"I cannot be antisemitic, because – look – some Jews agree with me" is a fallacious, ridiculous and actually offensive "argument".

'Classic' antisemitic tropes

Most Jews have no difficulty recognising certain stereotypes, which have been historically associated with anti-Jewish prejudice.

The 'blood libel' (the claim that Jews murder children and use their blood in Passover bread or other ritual uses) is a particularly old and vile accusation, which has been used for centuries to demonise Jews and make possible horrific atrocities against them. It is hard not to see echoes of that trope in articles and caricatures depicting Israeli soldiers, Israeli politicians and the Israeli society in general as blood-thirsty monsters that **deliberately** kill children. Google "caricature Netanyahu kills children" and one will be flooded with horrific depictions of the Israeli Prime Minister killing children. Substitute "Netanyahu" with the name of outrageous butchers like "Assad" or "Omar al-Bashir" and one finds less bloody caricatures and much less use of children.

Medieval tropes made Jews responsible for the spread of deadly diseases and for poisoning water wells. Both tropes find a (merely coincidental?) echo in accusations against the Jewish state. [9, 10, 11]

Another medieval trope is that Jews have a characteristic odour, some sort of demonic smell. This, too, occasionally finds "modern" reverberations. [12, 13, 14]

A very pervasive antisemitic prejudice is that portraying Jews as rich, dishonest in money matters, greedy and avaricious. Ken Livingstone appears to harbour such prejudice. [15, 16]

Yet another pervasive myth is that of "the Jewish conspiracy" – an all-powerful Jewish

171

cabal controlling or attempting to control countries, powerful corporations, or "the world". This is an age-old but very persistent prejudice, reflected in the "Elders of Zion" forgery and also used by Nazi propaganda. This deeply entrenched conspiracy theory finds its "modern" outlets in "Jewish lobby" accusations [17, 18, 19, 20, 21]. That perpetrators of such conspiracy theories sometimes use euphemisms like "Zionist lobby" or "Israel lobby" does not change the essence of the message. The issue is not whether Jews "lobby" or not. Of course they do lobby governments, parliaments and other authorities, in support of their interests. All communities do. The issue is also not whether Jews do their lobbying (on Israel and other issues of interest) better or worse than other communities. The suggestion (sometimes clearly expressed, otherwise just implied) is that Jewish lobbying is somehow "special", dishonest, conspiratorial, ill-intentioned.

A very strong example of the use of the "Jewish conspiracy" canard in the context of the Arab-Israeli conflict is the Covenant of

Hamas. Here is an interesting passage in
Article 22:
*"For a long time, the enemies have been
planning, skilfully and with precision, for the
achievement of what they have attained. They
took into consideration the causes affecting
the current of events. They strived to amass
great and substantive material wealth which
they devoted to the realisation of their dream.
With their money, they took control of the
world media, news agencies, the press,
publishing houses, broadcasting stations, and
others. With their money they stirred
revolutions in various parts of the world with
the purpose of achieving their interests and
reaping the fruit therein. They were behind the
French Revolution, the Communist revolution
and most of the revolutions we heard and hear
about, here and there. With their money they
formed secret societies, such as Freemasons,
Rotary Clubs, the Lions and others in different
parts of the world for the purpose of
sabotaging societies and achieving Zionist
interests. With their money they were able to
control imperialistic countries and instigate
them to colonize many countries in order to*

173

enable them to exploit their resources and spread corruption there.

You may speak as much as you want about regional and world wars. They were behind World War I, when they were able to destroy the Islamic Caliphate, making financial gains and controlling resources. They obtained the Balfour Declaration, formed the League of Nations through which they could rule the world. They were behind World War II, through which they made huge financial gains by trading in armaments, and paved the way for the establishment of their state. It was they who instigated the replacement of the League of Nations with the United Nations and the Security Council to enable them to rule the world through them. There is no war going on anywhere, without having their finger in it.

'So often as they shall kindle a fire for war, Allah shall extinguish it; and they shall set their minds to act corruptly in the earth, but Allah loveth not the corrupt doers.' (The Table - verse 64).

The imperialistic forces in the Capitalist West and Communist East, support the enemy with all their might, in money and in men. These forces take turns in doing that. The day Islam

174

appears, the forces of infidelity would unite to challenge it, for the infidels are of one nation."

This is the constitutive document of the organisation whose leaders Jeremy Corbyn has described as 'friends'. What would be the Labour Party's reaction, if the leader of Israel's main opposition party would call Ku Klux Klan leaders 'friends'?

'New' antisemitic tropes

Although 'new' in chronological sense, these antisemitic views are related and in fact are extensions of the 'old' ones.

A 'family' of such antisemitic beliefs are Holocaust-related. The most basic one is Holocaust denial. This is built, among other things on the old "conspiracy" trope: if the Holocaust never happened, then some sort of Jewish cabal or 'lobby' invented it for very ignoble purposes. There are several variants of Holocaust denial, besides "never happened": that it was "exaggerated" [22]; that the Jews themselves (or "the Zionists") have somehow concocted it or been complicit in it (see [23] and [24]); that it was brought about by the Jews' own faults (see [25]).

An even more pernicious version is Holocaust inversion: the claim that "what Israel is doing to Palestinians" is comparable, similar or even identical or worse than what the Nazis did to the Jews (see [26, 27, 28]). . Beyond the factual incompatibility of the situations, it should be noted that the Nazi comparison is rarely employed when Jews (or the Jewish state) are not involved.
Nazism has come to be identified as the symbol of evil; the comparison with the Jewish state is an extension of the old "Jew/demon/monster" theme.

A variant of that accusation is "apartheid" – another regime that entered history as a symbol of evil. On a personal note: I get a bit sad whenever I hear or read the accusation of apartheid levelled against Israel. Not just because I sense the profound prejudice that lurks behind such accusation, but because it reminds me of my father, who passed away in Jerusalem's Hadassah Medical Centre in March 2006. He lost the battle with cancer –

despite the heroic efforts of the hospital's staff (both Arabs and Jews), led by the Head of Surgery Department, Prof. Ahmed Eid, himself a Jerusalemite Arab. My father spent his last days in the ICU unit, sharing a cubicle with a young Palestinian from the West Bank town of Kalkilia, who had fallen off a scaffold. Some apartheid!

Needless to say, the accusation of apartheid is also very rarely employed, except for the Jewish state.

Double standards

As a result of antisemitic prejudice, historically Jews have suffered from legal and societal discrimination. Jews were judged using a different yardstick. In one of his books, Prof. Alan Dershowitz recalls the notoriously anti-Semitic early 20th century president of Harvard University, A. Lawrence Lowell. When asked why he singled Jews out for low admission quotas, Lowell claimed that, "Jewish students cheat." A member of staff reminded Lowell that non-Jewish students were also caught cheating. Lowell retorted:

177

"You're changing the subject. We are talking about Jews now."

Most Jews see the Jewish state being treated in a similar way. A classic example is the issue of Israeli **settlements** in the West Bank. Of course, it is perfectly legitimate to criticise those settlements, point out that they are illegal (even though legal experts are by no means unanimous about that), etc. The problem is that people who seem to spend half of their time ranting about Israeli settlements have nothing to say about settlements in other occupied territories: Western Sahara [29], North Cyprus [30], Tibet [31], etc. It seems that asking people to apply the same standard to all settlements is "changing the subject" away from the Jewish state!

A similar attitude appears to govern some people's assessment of Gaza-Israel conflicts: while the proportion of **Palestinian civilians** killed is repeated ad nauseam, it is never compared to that registered in other recent conflicts. It seems that the Jewish state is measured using a dedicated yardstick, one not employed for any other nation.

It is only the Jewish state, it seems, whose very **right to exist** (and to have a specific character imparted by the majority of its inhabitants) is constantly questioned – to the point where people do not shy away from suggesting ethnic cleansing [32] of Israeli Jews as the "solution". This is also the solution favoured by Mr. Corbyn's 'friends' from Hamas. In the introduction of their Covenant, they claim:
"Israel will exist and will continue to exist until Islam will obliterate it, just as it obliterated others before it"

I wonder what Mr. Corbyn would say if Benjamin Netanyahu would propose to 'obliterate' or 'relocate' Palestine to – say – Saudi Arabia?

A particularly venomous way to contest Israel's right to exist is to declare it a "**settler colonialist**" enterprise, i.e. to put it in the same category with the colonisation and settlement by Europeans of South Africa,

179

North and South America, Australia, etc. In addition to being extremely offensive to most Jews, the suggestion is intellectually dishonest. I have discussed previously the centrality of the Land of Israel in Jewish religion and culture and the long history of Zionism. Jews who went to settle in Mandatory and pre-Mandatory Palestine were not driven by imperialist and colonialist agendas. They were re-settling in their ancestral homeland. This was no colonial enterprise, but one of national emancipation and independence.

Historically, **boycotts** have constituted one of the major manifestations of systematic discrimination against Jews. This culminated with the Nazi-organised boycott of Jewish businesses remembered by its German name (Judenboycott) and slogan (Kauft nicht bei Juden). To most Jews, the call to single out the Jewish state (and only the Jewish state) for this type of "cruel and unusual punishment" is a chilly reminder of that boycott. The uniquely intense rage manifested by 'protesters' against Israeli businesses, artists, academics that have nothing to do with politics or with military conflict is a stark reminder of the Nazi-organised mobs that 'demonstrated' against Jewish businesses, artists and professionals. It should be noted that there are few calls (and even less organised actions) to boycott any other country, including the most egregious human rights violators. People drive to anti-Israel protests in their cars fuelled with Saudi petrol!

Freedom of speech
It has been claimed that taking steps to tackle antisemitism (for instance, by excluding members who have expressed antisemitic prejudice) constitutes a limitation of freedom of speech.

This is a fallacy. Freedom of speech (even speech that causes offence) is a fundamental human right; while necessary sometimes, its limitations should be kept minimal. However, excluding people from an organisation does not muzzle them. Ken Livingston did not lose his right of free speech just because he has been suspended from the Labour Party. In reality, we are not talking about freedom of speech, but about freedom to be a member of

181

a political party irrespective of one's opinions and behaviour. Such a right does not exist – nor should it exist. Membership in any organisation is governed by the principles of that organisation – it is not an absolute right. Since the Labour Party enshrines anti-racism among its principles, it should exclude people who manifest racism.

Suggestions

Here are my suggestions:

- That the Labour Party leadership officially declares zero tolerance towards manifestations of antisemitism and other forms of racism, in whatever shape and under whatever disguise they come;

- That the Labour Party leadership officially acknowledges that members of racist and terrorist organisations such as Hamas and Hezbollah are not 'friends' and that calling them such was a mistake;

- That the Labour Party leadership officially acknowledges that critical discourse about Israel (including within the Party) has slipped into the realm of antisemitism and that this needs to be redressed;

\-   That the Labour Party leadership reaffirms that Israel has the right to exist as the state of the Jewish people, in security and at peace with its neighbours;

\-   That the Labour Party leadership invites the Board of Deputies to draw up a definition of antisemitism based on the collective views of the British Jewish community and to put together an education programme for Labour activists, aimed at recognising and eliminating anti-Jewish prejudice.

Yours sincerely,
Noru Tsalic

Editor's note:
This is the only acknowledgment received by Noru:
Thank you for emailing the Chakrabarti Inquiry. <u>Please do not reply to this email</u>. This email is to acknowledge that the Inquiry has received your email. We apologise for not being able to provide individual acknowledgements of responses to the Inquiry due to the volume of responses. This email is

regularly monitored and all responses
received by 10 June 2016 will be considered.

References
[1] http://freespeechonisrael.org.uk/shami-chakrabarti-inquiry-remit-make-submission/
[2] https://www.thejc.com/news/uk-news/israel-attitudes-survey-most-are-happy-to-be-zionists-1.16850
[3]
https://www.youtube.com/watch?v=qPROXhnoUm8
[4] https://www.palestinecampaign.org/wp-content/uploads/disappearing-palestine-A3-poster-PRINT-Jan-2014.pdf
[5]
http://www.telegraph.co.uk/news/2016/05/03/ken-livingstone-and-the-hard-left-are-spreading-the-insidious-vi/
[6] http://rabbisacks.org/anti-zionism-is-the-new-anti-semitism-rabbi-sacks-writes-for-newsweek/

[7]
http://www.aaregistry.org/historic_events/vie
w/nigger-word-brief-history
[8]
https://engageonline.wordpress.com/2010/10
/12/jacobsons-demolition-of-the-ashamed-
jews-wins-man-booker/
[9] http://www.jpost.com/Arab-Israeli-
Conflict/World-Health-Organization-
condemnation-of-Israel-is-anti-Semitism-says-
Lapid-455124
[10]
http://www.algemeiner.com/2016/01/04/pale
stinian-news-agency-alleges-israel-
responsible-for-cancer-in-gaza-west-bank/
[11]
http://mondoweiss.net/2016/03/palestinians-
in-gaza-are-drinking-contaminated-water-
from-their-sinks/
[12]
http://www.independent.co.uk/voices/comm
entators/johann-hari/johann-hari-israel-is-
suppressing-a-secret-it-must-face-
816661.html
[13]
http://news.bbc.co.uk/1/hi/world/europe/172
1172.stm

[14]
http://www.washingtontimes.com/news/2016/apr/21/harvard-law-student-asks-tzipi-livni-israeli-polit/

[15]
http://www.telegraph.co.uk/news/politics/10813331/Jews-vote-Tory-because-they-are-rich-Ken-Livingstone-says.html

[16]
http://www.telegraph.co.uk/news/religion/9158948/Ken-Livingstone-accused-of-rich-Jews-remark.html

[17]
http://www.independent.co.uk/news/uk/politics/labour-mp-gerald-kaufman-accuses-government-of-being-swayed-by-jewish-money-a6712796.html

[18] http://www.thejc.com/news/uk-news/board-attacks-tonge%E2%80%99s-israel-lobby-criticism

[19]
https://electronicintifada.net/content/how-israel-lobby-manufactured-uk-labour-partys-anti-semitism-crisis/16481

[20]
http://www.independent.co.uk/voices/comm

ent/the-truth-about-the-uks-powerful-jewish-
lobbies-9702262.html
[21] http://davidduke.com/inside-jewish-
lobby-americas-powerful-organization/
[22]
http://www.economist.com/node/7912959
[23]
http://www.tabletmag.com/scroll/170686/ma
hmoud-abbas-still-a-holocaust-denier
[24]
http://www.independent.co.uk/news/world/
world-history/adolf-hitler-zionism-zionist-
nazis-haavara-agreement-ken-livingstone-
labour-antisemitism-row-a7009981.html
[25] http://www.dailymail.co.uk/news/article-
3531852/Labour-councillor-20-suspended-
claims-called-Hitler-greatest-man-history-
latest-anti-Semitic-scandal-hit-Corbyn-s-
party.html
[26]
http://www.theguardian.com/commentisfree/
2016/mar/15/antisemitism-israel-policies-
labour-activist-vicki-kirby
[27]
http://www.haaretz.com/jewish/news/british-
mp-compares-jewish-treatment-of-
palestinians-to-nazis.premium-1.496504

[28] http://www.pol-inc-pol.com/2014/07/john-scumbag-prescott.html

[29] http://www.aljazeera.com/indepth/features/2012/12/201212247936401443.html

[30] http://www.telegraph.co.uk/news/worldnews/europe/cyprus/1406583/Turkish-Cypriots-leave-island-as-settlers-move-in.html

[31] https://www.theguardian.com/world/2008/may/24/tibet.china

[32] http://www.independent.co.uk/news/uk/politics/labour-mp-naz-shah-apologises-for-backing-relocate-israel-to-north-america-plan-a7001406.html

Jonathan Turner's Submission
Barrister and Chair of UK Lawyers for Israel

Dear Ms Chakrabarti and Prof. Feldman
I attach an excerpt from Paul Johnson's book
"A History of the Jews" which I think sheds
valuable light on the relationship between
anti-Semitism and antizionism.
Yours sincerely
Jonathan Turner

**Extract from Paul Johnson's 'A History of the
Jews' showing the history of left wing anti-
Semitism**

The Soviet campaign against the Jews, after
1967 a permanent feature of the system, was
itself conducted under the code-name of anti-
Zionism, which became a cover for every
variety of anti-Semitism. Soviet anti-Zionism, a
product of internal divisions within the east
European Jewish left, was in turn grafted on to
Leninist anti-imperialism. At this point we
need to retrace our steps a little, in order to
show that the Leninist theory of imperialism,
like Marx's theory of capitalism, had its roots
in anti-Semitic conspiracy theory.

189

The theory arose from the development of South Africa from the 1860s onwards, the outstanding example of the application of large-scale capital to transform a primitive into a modern economy. South Africa had been a rural backwater until the discovery of the diamond fields of Kimberley in the 1860s, followed by the goldfields of the Rand twenty years later, opened up its interior and mineral wealth. What made South Africa different was the use of a new institution, the mining finance house, to concentrate claims and to raise and deploy enormous capital sums in high-technology deep mining. The institution itself was invented by an Englishman, Cecil Rhodes. But Jews had always been involved in precious stones (especially diamonds) and bullion, and they played a notable part both in the South African deep-level mines and in the financial system which raised the capital to sink them. Such men as Alfred Beit, Barney Barnato, Louis Cohen, Lionel Phillips, Julius Wehrner, Solly Joel, Adolf Goertz, George Albu and Abe Bailey turned South Africa into the world's largest and richest mining economy. A second generation of mining financiers, led by

Ernest Oppenheimer, consolidated and expanded the achievement.

The rapid fortunes made (and sometimes lost) on the Rand by Jews aroused great jealousy and resentment. Among their critics was the left-wing polemicist J.A. Hobson, who went out to South Africa to cover the outbreak of the Boer War in 1899 for the Manchester Guardian. Hobson regarded the Jew as 'almost devoid of social morality', possessing a 'superior calculating intellect, which is a national heritage' allowing him 'to take advantage of every weakness, folly and vice of the society in which he lives'. In South Africa he was shocked and angered by what he saw as the ubiquitous activity of Jews. The official figures, he wrote, stated there were only 7,000 Jews in Johannesburg but 'The shop fronts and business houses, the market place, the saloons, the "stoops" of the smart suburban houses are sufficient to convince one of the large presence of the chosen people.' He was particularly disgusted to find that the stock exchange was closed on the Day of Atonement. In 1900 he published a book 'The War in South Africa: Its Causes and

Effects', which blamed the war on 'a small group of international financiers, chiefly German in origin and Jewish by race'. British troops were fighting and dying 'in order to place a small international oligarchy of mine-owners and speculators in power in Pretoria'. 'Not Hamburg,' he wrote in disgust, 'not Vienna, not Frankfurt but Johannesburg is the new Jerusalem.'

Hobson's explanation of the origin of the war was false. The fighting, as was foreseeable, was disastrous for the mine-owners. As for the Jews, the whole of modern history proved them strongly pacific by inclination and interest, especially in their capacity as financiers. But Hobson, like other conspiracy theorists, was not interested in facts but in the beauty of his concept. Two years later he expanded his theory into a famous book, 'Imperialism: A Study', which revealed international finance capital as the chief force behind colonies and wars. His chapter, 'Economic Parasites of Imperialism', the heart of his theory, contained this key passage: 'Those great businesses – banking, brokering, bill discounting, loan floating, company promoting – form the central ganglion of international capitalism. United by the strongest bonds of organization, always in closest and quickest touch with one another, situated in the very heart of the business capital of every state, controlled, so far as Europe is concerned, chiefly by men of a single and peculiar race, who have behind them many centuries of financial experience, they are in a unique position to control the policy of nations. No great quick direction of capital is possible save by their consent and through their agency. Does anyone seriously suppose that a great war could be undertaken by any European state, or a great state loan subscribed, if the house of Rothschild and its connections set their face against it?'

When Lenin came to write his own thesis on the subject, at Zurich in the spring of 1916, he complained of a shortage of books. 'However,' he wrote, 'I made use of the principal English work on imperialism, J.A. Hobson's book, with all the care that, in my opinion, this work deserves.' Hobsons's theory, in fact, became the essence of Lenin's own. The result, 'Imperialism: The Highest Stage of Capitalism' (1916) laid down the standard doctrine on the subject for all states under Communism, from 1917 to the present day. Leninist theory, in one form or another, likewise formed the attitudes of many Third World states towards imperialism and colonialism, as they acquired independence in the 1950s and 1960s.

Granted the theory's anti-Semitic roots, it was not difficult to fit into it the concept of Zionism as a form of colonialism and the Zionist state as an outpost of imperialism. There were, it was true, the awkward historical facts of Israel's birth, with Stalin acting as one of the principal midwives. These in themselves demolished the Soviet theory of Zionism completely. But like many other facts in Soviet history, they were buried and forgotten by the official propagandists. In any case the entire history of anti-Semitism demonstrates how impervious it is to awkward facts. That 'Zionism' in practice stood for 'the Jews' became quickly apparent. The 1952 Slansky trial was the first occasion in the history of Communism that the traditional anti-Semitic accusation of a world-wide Jewish conspiracy, with the American Jewish Joint Distribution

Committee and the Israeli government constituting the modern Elders of Zion, was put forward officially by a Communist government – an ominous milestone. The reality behind the scenes was even worse. The Jewish Deputy Foreign Minister Artur London, sentenced to life imprisonment but released in the 'Prague Spring' of 1968, was then able to reveal the anti-Semitic fury of the chief prosecutor, Major Smole: '(He) took me by the throat and in a voice shaking with hatred shouted: "You and your dirty race, we shall exterminate it. Not everything Hitler did was right. But he exterminated Jews and that was a good thing. Far too many of them managed to avoid the gas chamber but we shall finish where he left off."'

From the early 1950s, Soviet anti-Zionist propaganda, growing steadily in intensity and comprehensiveness, stressed the links between Zionism, the Jews in general, and Judaism. 'Judaic sermons are the sermons of bourgeois Zionists', announced a Ukrainian-language broadcast from Korovograd, 9 December 1959. 'The character of the Jewish religion', the Kuibyshev newspaper

Volszhskaya Kommuna wrote on 30 September 1961, 'serves the political aims of the Zionists.' 'Zionism', wrote Kommunist Moldavia in 1963, 'is inseparably linked to Judaism...rooted in the idea of the exclusiveness of the Jewish people.' Hundreds of articles, in magazines and newspapers all over the Soviet Union, portrayed Zionists (i.e. Jews) and Israeli leaders as engaged in a world-wide conspiracy, along the lines of the old Protocols of Zion. It was, Sovietskaya Latvia wrote, 5 August 1967, an 'international Cosa Nostra' with a 'common centre, a common programme and common funds'. The 'Israeli ruling circles' were only junior partners in its global plots.

In the twenty years after the 1967 Six Day War, the Soviet propaganda machine became the main source for anti-Semitic material in the world. In doing so it assembled materials from virtually every archaeological layer of anti-Semitic history, from classical antiquity to Hitlerism. The sheer volume of the material, ranging from endlessly repetitive articles and broadcasts to full-scale books, began to rival the Nazi output. Trofim Kychko's book,

'Judaism and Zionism' (1968) spoke of the 'chauvinistic idea of the God-chosenness of the Jewish people, the propaganda of messianism and the idea of ruling over the peoples of the world'. Vladimir Begun's 'Creeping Counter-Revolution' (1974) called the Bible 'an unsurpassed textbook of bloodthirstiness, hypocrisy, treason, perfidy and moral degeneracy'; no wonder the Zionists were gangsters since their ideas came from 'the scrolls of the "holy" Torah and the precepts of the Talmud'. In 1972 the Soviet embassy journal in Paris actually reproduced parts of a Tsarist anti-Semitic pamphlet put out in 1906 by the Black Hundred, who organized the pre-1914 pogroms. In this instance it was possible to take action in the French courts, which duly found the publisher (a prominent member of the French Communist Party) guilty of incitement to racial violence. Some of the Soviet anti-Semitic material, circulated at a very high level, almost defied belief. In a Central Committee memorandum of 10 January 1977, one Soviet anti-Semitic expert, Valery Emelianov, claimed that America was controlled by a Zionist-masonic conspiracy ostensibly led by President

Carter but actually under the control of what he called the 'B'nai Brith Gestapo'. The Zionists, according to Emelianov, penetrated goy society through the masons, each one of whom was an active Zionist informer; Zionism itself was based on "the Judaic-masonic pyramid. "

The keystone of the new Soviet fantasy-edifice of anti-Semitism was provided in the 1970s, when the charge that the Zionists were the racist successors of the Nazis was 'proved' by 'evidence' that Hitler's Holocaust itself was a Jewish-Nazi conspiracy to get rid of poor Jews who could not be used in Zionist plans. Indeed, it was alleged, Hitler himself got his ideas from Herzl. The Jewish-Zionist leaders, acting on orders from the millionaire Jews who controlled international finance capital, helped the ss and the Gestapo to herd unwanted Jews either into the gas ovens or into the kibbutzim of the Land of Canaan. This Jewish-Nazi conspiracy was used as background by the Soviet propaganda machine to charges of atrocities against the Israeli government, especially during and after the Lebanon operations of 1982. Since the Zionists were happy to join with Hitler in exterminating their own discarded people, wrote Pravda on 17 January 1984, it was not surprising that they were now massacring Lebanese Arabs, whom they regarded as sub-human anyway.

These sinister developments in the anti-Semitic policy of the Soviet government were more than a reversion to traditional Tsarist practice, though they included most of the familiar Tsarist mythology about Jews. For one thing, Tsarist governments always allowed the Jews escape through mass emigration. For another, the Soviet regime had a record second only to Hitler's in exterminating entire categories of people for ideological purposes. The equation of Jews with Zionism, a capital offence in Soviet doctrine, would make it the easiest thing in the world for the Soviet leadership to justify in ideological terms extreme measures against Russia's 1,750,000 Jews, such as reviving Stalin's 1952-3 plan to deport them en masse to Siberia, or even worse.

Another disturbing factor was the close resemblance between Soviet anti-Jewish propaganda and similar material put out by Russian's allies in the Arab world. The difference was more of form than of substance. The Arabs were less thorough in their use of ideological jargon and they sometimes openly used the word 'Jew' where the Russians were usually careful to employ the code-term 'Zionists'. Where the Russians drew from the 'Protocols of Zion' without acknowledgment, the Arabs published it openly. This tract had circulated widely in the Arab world, published in innumerable different editions, ever since the early 1920s. It was read by such diverse Arab leaders as King Feisal of Saudi Arabia and President Nasser of Egypt. The latter evidently believed it, telling an Indian journalist in 1957: 'It is very important that you should read it. I will give you a copy. It proves beyond a shadow of a doubt that three hundred Zionists, each of whom knows all the others, govern the fate of the European continent and that they elect their successors from their entourage.' Nasser was so impressed by the book that yet another Arab edition was published by his brother in about 1967. Extracts and summaries were used in Arab school

200

textbooks, and in training material for the Arab armed forces. In 1972 yet another edition of it appeared at the top of the Beirut best-seller list.

All these editions, it should be added, were specially edited for Arab readers and the Elders were presented in the context of the Palestine problem. The 'Protocols' were not the only anti-Semitic classic to live on in the post-war Arab world. Blood-libel material, published in Cairo in 1890 under the title 'The Cry of the Innocent in the Horn of Freedom', resurfaced in 1962 as an official publication of the UAR government called 'Talmudic Human Sacrifices'. Indeed the blood libel periodically reappeared in Arab newspapers. But the 'Protocols' remained the favourite, and not only in Arab Islamic countries. It was published in Pakistan in 1967 and extensive use was made of it by the Iranian government and its embassies after the Ayatollah Khomeini, a fervent believer in anti-Jewish conspiracy theory, came to power there in 1979. In May 1984, his publication 'Imam', which had already printed extracts from the 'Protocols', accused the British task force in the Falklands of conducting atrocities on the advice of the Elders of Zion. Khomeini's propaganda usually portrayed Zionism (alias the Jews), which had been at work 'for centuries everywhere, perpetrating crimes of unbelievable magnitude against human societies and values', as an emanation of Satan. Khomeini followed the medieval line that Jews were sub-human or inhuman, indeed anti-human, and therefore constituted an exterminable category of creature. But his anti-Semitism hovered confusingly between simple anti-Judaism, Islamic sectarianism (Sunni Moslems ruling his enemy Iraq were Zionist puppets as well as devils in their own right) and hatred of America, 'the Great Satan'. He found it difficult to decide whether Satan was manipulating Washington via the Jews or vice versa.

Arab anti-Semitism too was uneasy blend of religious and secular motifs. It was also ambivalent about the role of Hitler and the Nazis. The Grand Mufti of Jerusalem had known of the Final Solution and welcomed it. Hitler told him that when his troops reached the Middle East they would wipe out the

Jewish settlements in Palestine. After the war, many Arabs continued to regard Hitler as a hero-figure. When Eichmann was brought to trial in 1961-2, the English-language Jordanian newspaper, Jerusalem Times, published a letter congratulating him for having 'conferred a real blessing on humanity'. The trial would 'one day culminate in the liquidation of the remaining six million to avenge your blood.' On the other hand, Arab anti-Semitic propagandists often followed the Soviet line that Jews and Nazis had worked hand-in-glove, and that the Zionists were the Nazis' natural successors. Particularly in their propaganda directed at the West, Arab governments compared the Israeli air force to the Luftwaffe and the IDF to the SS and Gestapo. At one time or another (sometimes simultaneously) Arab audiences were informed that the Holocaust had been a fortunate event, a diabolical plot between Jews and Nazis, and had never occurred at all, being a simple invention of the Zionists. But when had anti-Semitic theorists ever been disturbed by internal contradictions in their assertions?

The quantity of anti-Zionist material flooding into the world, from both the Soviet bloc and the Arab states, was augmented first by the 1967 Six Day War, which acted as a powerful stimulant to Soviet propaganda against Israel, then by the oil-price revolution following the 1973 Yom Kippur War, which greatly increased Arab funds made available for anti-Zionist propaganda.

Inevitably the scale and persistence of anti-Israeli abuse had some effect, notably in the United Nations. The old League of Nations had shown itself singularly ineffective in protecting Jews during the inter-war period. But at least it had not actively encouraged their persecution. The 1975 session of the United Nations General Assembly came close to legitimizing anti-Semitism. On 1 October it received in state President Idi Amin of Uganda, in his capacity as Chairman of the Organization of African Unity. Amin was already notorious for his large-scale massacres of the Ugandan population, some of which he had carried out personally. He was also well known for the violence of his anti-Semitic statements. He had sent a cable to the UN secretary-general

on 12 September 1972 applauding the
Holocaust, and he announced that, since no
statue to Hitler had been erected in Germany,
he proposed to set one up in Uganda. Despite
this, or perhaps because of it, he was well
received by the General Assembly. Many UN
delegates, including the whole of the Soviet
and Arab blocs, gave him a standing ovation
before he began his speech, in which he
denounced the 'Zionist-American conspiracy'
against the world and called for the expulsion
of Israel from the UN and its 'extinction'.
There was frequent applause during his
grotesque philippic and another standing
ovation when he sat down. The following day
the UN secretary-general and the president of
the General Assembly gave a public dinner in
his honour. A fortnight later, on 17 October,
the professional anti-Semites of the Soviet and
Arab publicity machines achieved their
greatest triumphs when the Third Committee
of the General Assembly, by a vote of 70 to 29,
with 27 abstentions and 16 absent, passed a
motion condemning Zionism as a form of
racism. On 10 November the General
Assembly as a whole endorsed the resolution
by 67 to 55 with 15 abstentions. The Israeli

delegate, Chaim Herzog, pointed out that the vote took place on the thirty-seventh anniversary of the Nazi Kristallnacht against the Jews. The US delegate, Daniel P. Moynihan, announced with icy contempt: 'The United States rises to declare before the General Assembly of the United Nations, and before the world, that it does not acknowledge, it will not abide by, and it will never acquiesce in this infamous act.'

One of the principal lessons of Jewish history has been that repeated verbal slanders are sooner or later followed by violent physical deeds. Time and again over the centuries, anti-Semitic writings created their own fearful momentum which climaxed in an effusion of Jewish blood. The Hitlerian Final Solution was unique in its atrocity but it was none the less prefigured in nineteenth-century anti-Semitic theory. The anti-Semitic torrent poured out by the Soviet bloc and the Arab states in the post-war period produced its own characteristic form of violence: state-sponsored terrorism. There was irony in this weapon being used against Zionism, for it was militant Zionists, such as Avraham Stern and

Menachem Begin, who had (it could be argued) invented terrorism in its modern, highly organized and scientific form. That it should be directed, on a vastly increased scale, against the state they had lived, and died, to create could be seen as an act of providential retribution or at any rate as yet another demonstration that idealists who justified their means by their ends did so at their peril. The age of international terrorism, created by post-war Soviet-Arab anti-Semitism, effectively opened in 1968 when the Palestine Liberation Organization formally adopted terror and mass murder as its primary policy. The PLO, and its various competitors and imitators , directed their attacks primarily against Israeli targets but they made no attempt to distinguish between Israeli citizens, or Zionists, and Jews, any more than traditional anti-Semitic killers distinguished between religious Jews and Jews by birth. When members of the Baader-Meinhof gang, a German fascist left organization inspired by Soviet anti-Semitic propaganda, hijacked an Air France aircraft flying from Paris to Tel Aviv on 27 June 1976, and forced it to land in Idi Amin's Uganda, the terrorists carefully separated the non-Jews from the Jews, who were taken aside to be murdered. One of those they planned to kill still had the SS concentration camp number tattooed on his arm.

Judy Weleminsky's Submission.
Founder Pro Israel, Pro Palestine,
Pro Peace

Dear Shami Chakrabarti.

I was a long term active member of Labour
because I believe in promoting social justice. I
left in 2004 due to observing some disturbing
behaviour and policies which went against
social justice. While these were not directly
related to anti-Semitism I believe they are
connected in that principle was trampled in
pursuit of powerful non social justice interests.

I continued until recently to be a supporter on
the basis that Labour were better than the
opposition. However, the writing was on the
wall for me when Ed Miliband equated his
condemnation of Hamas terrorist rocket
attacks on Israel with the Israeli response to
try and prevent such attacks. It was the
equivalent of a murderer being equated with
the police trying to prevent murder. It became
clear that the justice issue in the situation was
subservient to perceived political advantage

209

and the pressure from anti-Israel lobbyists and pressure groups with much greater voting power.

Since then the rhetoric has ramped up and anti-Israel commentary has gained the upper hand in many parts of the Labour party. For me anti-Israel stances are anti-Semitic and indeed many comments have had both anti-Israel and anti-Semitic content. Labour needs to robustly tackle this issue in important parts of its activist groups and base and show quick and effective leadership – so far this has been missing.

With almost half the Jews in the world living in Israel and more than 80% of Jews having relatives there and 100% knowing that if things got bad in their current homes Israel is the only place guaranteed to welcome them, Israel is vital for the future of the Jewish people. Please do not be taken in by those who claim to be Jews and supporters of anti-Zionism. They are overwhelmingly people who have no future investment in the Jewish people. They do not have Jewish children and they do not support Jewish continuity initiatives. They are using/abusing their heritage to prove to the anti-Israel world that they are good guys.

I want to see robust leadership in changing the approach on the left of the party and recognising that many people from Muslim backgrounds have been schooled in anti-Semitism from an early age and this needs to be challenged and changed.

Yours

Judy Weleminsky

House of Commons Home Affairs Committee
Antisemitism in the UK
October 13 2016
Extract

113. While the Labour Leader has a proud record of campaigning against many types of racism, based on the evidence we have received, we are not persuaded that he fully appreciates the distinct nature of post-Second World War antisemitism. Unlike other forms of racism, antisemitic abuse often paints the victim as a malign and controlling force rather than as an inferior object of derision, making it perfectly possible for an 'anti-racist campaigner' to express antisemitic views. Jewish Labour MPs have been subject to appalling levels of abuse, including antisemitic death threats from individuals purporting to be supporters of Mr Corbyn. Clearly, the Labour Leader is not directly responsible for

abuse committed in his name, but we believe that his lack of consistent leadership on this issue, and his reluctance to separate antisemitism from other forms of racism, has created what some have referred to as a 'safe space' for those with vile attitudes towards Jewish people. This situation has been further exacerbated by the Party's demonstrable incompetence at dealing with members accused of antisemitism, as illustrated by the saga involving the suspension, re-admittance and re-suspension of Jackie Walker. The ongoing membership of Ken Livingstone, following his outbursts
about Hitler and Zionism, should also have been dealt with more effectively. The result is that the Labour Party, with its proud history of fighting racism and promoting equal rights, is seen by some as an unwelcoming place for Jewish members and activists.

114 .The decision by the Leader of the Labour Party to commission an independent inquiry into antisemitism was a welcome one, notwithstanding subsequent criticisms. The Chakrabarti report makes recommendations about creating a more robust disciplinary

213

process within the Labour Party, but it is clearly lacking in many areas; particularly in its failure to differentiate explicitly between racism and antisemitism. The fact that the report describes occurrences of antisemitism merely as "unhappy incidents" also suggests that it fails to appreciate the full gravity of the comments that prompted the inquiry in the first place. These shortfalls, combined with Ms Chakrabarti's decision to join the Labour Party in April and accept a peerage as a nominee of the Leader of that Party, and her subsequent appointment as Shadow Attorney General, have thrown into question her claims (and those of Mr Corbyn) that her inquiry was truly independent. Ms Chakrabarti has not been sufficiently open with the Committee about when she was offered her peerage, despite several attempts to clarify this issue with her. It is disappointing that she did not foresee that the timing of her elevation to the House of Lords, alongside a report absolving the Labour Leader of any responsibility for allegations of increased antisemitism within his Party, would completely undermine her efforts to address this issue. It is equally concerning that Mr Corbyn did not consider the damaging

214

impression likely to be created by this sequence of events.

115. The recommendations of the Chakrabarti report are further impaired by the fact that they are not accompanied by a clear definition of antisemitism, as we have recommended should be adopted by all political parties. We remain unconvinced of the robustness of the Labour Party's code of conduct (and whether it will be effectively enforced), and the report does nothing to address a severe lack of transparency within the Party's disciplinary process. There are examples of Labour members who have been accused of antisemitism, investigated by their Party, and then reinstated with no explanation of why their behaviour was not deemed to be antisemitic. The Labour Party, and all other political parties in the same circumstances, should publish a clear public statement alongside every reinstatement or expulsion of a member after any investigation into suspected antisemitism.

116. We see no good reason for the Chakrabarti report's proposed statute of

limitations on antisemitic misdemeanours. Antisemitism is not a new concept: an abusive, antisemitic tweet sent in 2013 is no more defensible than one sent in 2016. If the Labour Party or any other organisation is to demonstrate that it is serious about antisemitism, it should investigate all allegations with equal seriousness, regardless of when the behaviour is alleged to have taken place.

117. In its determination to be inclusive of all forms of racism, some sections of the Chakrabarti report do not acknowledge Jewish concerns, including its recommendations on training, which make no mention of antisemitism. This has generated criticism among some observers that antisemitism may be excluded from future training programmes. The Labour Party and all political parties should ensure that their training on racism and inclusivity features substantial sections on antisemitism. This must be formulated in consultation with Jewish community representatives, and must acknowledge the unique nature of antisemitism. If antisemitism is subsumed into a generic approach to

216

racism, its distinctive and dangerous characteristics will be overlooked. In addition, the Labour Party's disciplinary process must acknowledge the fact that an individual's demonstrated opposition to other forms of racism does not negate the possibility that they hold antisemitic beliefs; nor does it neutralise any expression of these beliefs.

118. The Chakrabarti Report is ultimately compromised by its failure to deliver a comprehensive set of recommendations, to provide a definition of antisemitism, or to suggest effective ways of dealing with antisemitism. The failure of the Labour Party to deal consistently and effectively with antisemitic incidents in recent years risks lending force to allegations that elements of the Labour movement are institutionally antisemitic.

119. The historical inaccuracy of Ken Livingstone's remarks regarding Hitler and Zionism have been analysed elsewhere, and it is not the job of this Committee to deliver lessons in Nazi history, except to point out that Mr Livingstone has since admitted that it

was "rubbish" to refer to Hitler as a Zionist. Regardless of academic rigour, his decision to invoke Hitler in a debate about antisemitism and Zionism—in defence of a Facebook post comparing Israel with the Nazis—was unwise, offensive and provocative. In light of previous incidents in which he has made comments that have been interpreted as antisemitic, or especially offensive to Jewish people, we believe it likely that he knew that his comments would cause similar offence. The fact that he continues to defend his position casts serious doubt on whether he has sufficient understanding of the nature of contemporary antisemitism. In the words of Mr Corbyn, who described himself as his friend, we hope that Mr Livingstone will "mend his ways" without delay.

Contributors
Christine Achinger

University of Warwick

Christine Achinger is an associate professor
In the Department of German Studies. She
studied philosophy, literature, and physics in
Paris and Hamburg, where she also worked
at the concentration camp memorial site
Hamburg-Neuengamme and in the Institute
for the History of the German Jews. She com-
pleted an MA in gender and ethnic studies in
London and then moved on to Nottingham
to write a PhD on the intersection of colonial
discourses of Poland and constructions of
Jewishness, gender, and nation in 19th-cen-
tury Germany, as reflected in Gustav Freytag's
novel Soll und Haben(1855).

During her time at the Frankel Center, she
worked on a series of case studies tracing the
development of constructions of Jewishness
and femininity, and their connection to the
development of modern society, in German-
speaking Central European culture between
the late 18th and the early 20th century.

Luke Akehurst

has been Director of We Believe in Israel since 2011. We Believe in Israel is a BICOM initiative and is a broad coalition of over 13,000 supporters of Israel which focuses on developing a grassroots pro-Israel movement. Luke is not Jewish but has been a committed Zionist all his life. Outside of work he was a Hackney Councillor for 12 years, has stood for Parliament twice and served on the Labour Party National Executive Committee. He was previously an award-winning Director at global PR company Weber Shandwick.

Jonathan G Campbell

Senior Lecturer in Biblical Studies & Judaism in the University of Bristol in the UK. He has a wide range of teaching and research experience in the field of Jewish Studies pertaining to both the ancient and modern periods. He has recently been focusing on the issue of contemporary resurgent antisemitism, co-organizing (with Dr Lesley Klaff) the Bristol-Sheffield Hallam Colloquium on Contemporary Antisemitism that took place in the University of Bristol in September 2015, as well as a second follow-on colloquium that ran in Sheffield Hallam University in September 2016; the proceedings of both events are expected to be published in due course. Dr Campbell is particularly interested in the role of the sacred texts and traditions of Christianity in past and present negative attitudes toward Jews, including the increasing presence of anti-Israel activism in the mainstream churches of the 21st century.

Ric Cooper
Born 1957 Former shopkeeper (scion of Millett family) and small-time commercial property investor, now part-time archivist and genealogist. Educated at Winchester College and Leeds University (Philosophy, BA Hons). Ran 'Revive!'young adults' social club in Brighton in the late 1990s. Divorced, no children. Founding member of South Hants Science Fiction Group (1980) and Jewish Genealogical Society of Great Britain (1992). Deputy to Board of Deputies and JC stringer for Portsmouth and Southsea Hebrew Congregation. Enthusiast of genealogy, science-fiction, traditional jazz and real ale. Drek-fressing Zionist and scofflaw troll.

Baroness Ruth Deech
Former Principal of St Anne's College Oxford, Chair of the UK Human Fertilisation & Embryology Authority, BBC Governor, Rhodes Scholarships Trustee, Gresham Professor of Law, the first Independent Adjudicator for Higher Education for England and Wales, and Chair of the Bar Standards Board. She holds an honorary degree from Ben Gurion University, is a patron of the CST, a trustee of the Tel Aviv University Roth Institute for the Study of Antisemitism, and a member of the All Party Britain-Israel Group. She is a Bencher of the Inner Temple and was appointed Honorary Queen's Counsel 2013. She was created a life peer in 2005 and sits in the House of Lords as a crossbench legislator.

Robert Fine
 is Emeritus Professor of Sociology at the University of Warwick. He was founding chair of the European Sociological Association Network on Racism and Antisemitism and

222

founding director of the Warwick Social Theory Centre. He recently co-authored for Manchester University Press (2017) *Antisemitism and the left: on the return of the Jewish question.* Among his books are: *Cosmopolitanism* (Routledge 2007); *Political Investigations: Hegel, Marx, Arendt* (Routledge 2001); *Democracy and the Rule of Law: Marx's Critique of the Legal Form* (Pluto 1985, Blackburn 2002); and *Beyond Apartheid: Labour and Liberation (*Pluto 1991). He co-edited 'Hannah Arendt's On Revolution: Fifty Years After', *European Journal of Cultural and Political Sociology* (2015); 'Racism and Antisemitism in Contemporary Europe', *European Societies (*2012); and 'Natural law and Social Theory', *Journal of Classical Sociology* (2013).

Mark Gardner

Director of Communications and Deputy Chief
Executive of CST, Community Security Trust,
the charity representing British Jews on issues
of security, policing and antisemitism. Mark
has represented CST, British and European
Jewry in numerous hearings, conferences and
events, and has authored many articles on
antisemitism and related matters. Mark was
awarded a Police commendation in 1999 for
his work on behalf of all Londoners during the
Nazi nail bombing campaign."

Eve Garrard

Eve Garrard is a moral philosopher who is
currently Honorary Research Fellow in the
Department of Philosophy at Manchester
University. Prior to this she was for several
years Senior Lecturer in the Centre for
Professional Ethics at Keele University. She has
a long-standing interest in teaching philosophy
to those who don't have a background in the
subject, and worked part-time for many years
for the Open University. Her research
interests are in moral theory, bioethics, and
philosophical issues connected with the

concepts of evil and forgiveness. She has co-edited a book on moral philosophy and the Holocaust, co-authored a book on forgiveness, published various papers in bioethics, and is currently working on further papers on evil and on forgiveness.

Richard Gold

Richard Gold is an active member of Bury South Labour Party. He has been active in the campaign against antisemitism run by Engage and is on the Northwest committee of the Jewish Labour Movement.

David Hirsh

David has been in the sociology department at Goldsmiths since 2003. He studied Sociology at City University, London; he did an MA in Philosophy and Social Theory at Warwick; and he wrote his PhD there on Crimes Against Humanity and International Law.
He was the holder of the Sociological Review Fellowship which enabled him to write <u>Law against Genocide: cosmopolitan trials</u>. This book was awarded the British Sociological Association Philip Abrams Prize for the best

first book in sociology in 2004. By focusing on two trials from the International Criminal Tribunal for the former Yugoslavia, the trial of Andrei Sawoniuk for crimes committed during the Holocaust, and the David Irving libel case, the book comes to some tentative conclusions about the possibility of the emergence of cosmopolitan law.

David's new book, out in September 2017, is 'Contemporary Left Antisemitism'. It begins with a chapter on the Livingstone Formulation, a standard response which accuses Jews of raising the issue of antisemitism in bad faith only in order to silence criticism of Israel or to smear the left. It has two chapters about the rise of antizionist and antisemitic politics in the British Labour movement and two chapters about the campaign to exclude Israelis from the academic, cultural, sporting and economic life of humanity. It has a critique of antizionism and the apartheid analogy; it also looks at specifically Jewish antizionism; it examines case studies of openly antisemitic discourse which have emerged out of antizionism; it discusses struggles over *defining* antisemitism; and it thinks about specifically sociological approaches to understanding contemporary antisemitism. You can find David on facebook and he tweets @DavidHirsh

Research Interests

Contemporary antisemitism; crimes against humanity; totalitarianism and totalitarian movements; the new populism; democracy and critiques of democracy.

Teaching

David teaches a number of first year introductory lectures on our undergraduate sociology courses, he convenes the second year criminology core and he teaches a second-year option course, 'Crimes against Humanity'. He also teaches on the sociology of human rights at MA level and he supervises students at PhD level.

In 2006/7, David was a Research Fellow at Yale University.

David acted as an expert witness in *South African Jewish Board of Deputies v Bongani Masuku*, Johannesburg, Feb 2017 and in *South African Jewish Board of Deputies v Islamic Unity Convention*, Cape Town, 2012.

David is active in, and was a co-convenor of, Research Network 31 in the European

Sociological Association on *Racism, Antisemitism and Ethnic Relations*.

David was a member of Experts Forums at the Inter-parliamentary Conference on Combating Antisemitism, hosted by the Canadian Government, Ottawa, 2010, the London Conference for Combatting Antisemitism, London, 2009, and a number of Global Forums for Combating Antisemitism in Jerusalem.

Lesley D Klaff
senior lecturer in law at Sheffield Hallam University. She is editor of the *Journal of Contemporary Antisemitism*, Associate Editor of the *Journal for the Study of Antisemitism*, and is a member of the editorial board of the *International Journal of the Social Research Foundation.* She serves on the Academic Advisory Boards of both the Louis D Brandeis Center for Human Rights Under Law and the Berlin International Center for the Study of Antisemitism. She is also a member of UK Lawyers for Israel. She has published on campus antisemitism, Holocaust inversion, and antisemitism in the Labour Party. Antisemitism. She is also a member of UK Lawyers for Israel. She has published on

campus antisemitism, Holocaust inversion, and antisemitism in the Labour Party.

Research and associated activities over the last year.

Attended, following a personal invitation from BICOM, the 2015 UK-Israel Strategic Challenges Conference at Portcullis House, Westminster – July 2015.

Co-organised and co-hosted the first Bristol-Sheffield Hallam University Colloquium on Contemporary Antisemitism at Bristol University – September 2015

Paper delivered at the Bristol-Sheffield Hallam Colloquium on Contemporary Antisemitism – *Using s. 26 Equality Act 2010 to combat institutional antisemitism: a critical race perspective on Fraser v University and College Union* – September 2015.

Paper given at the Bristol-Sheffield Hallam Colloquium converted into a chapter of 6,000 words – September 2015 – March 2016: to be published in book of colloquium proceedings by Academic Studies Press, 2017. Book title is 'Unity and Diversity in Contemporary Antisemitism'.

Participated in a panel at the Battle of Ideas and presented a paper – A 'rumble' on religion: from Enlightenment tolerance to twenty-first-century offence – September 2015

Paper delivered at the Pears Institute for the Study of Contemporary Antisemitism, Birkbeck, University of London – *The Jews and the Left in Britain Today* – November, 2015

Paper delivered at BBC event in London before an audience of 600 + – *Does BBC Coverage of Israel Adversely Impact British Jews* – November, 2015. Coverage on my paper featured in the Jewish Chronicle and I was quoted. The BBC was asked to respond to my charge that it is institutionally antisemitism and it denied it (of course.)

Was appointed 'affiliate professor' of Haifa University for one year – December 2015.

Article – Israeli Aoartheid Week in Britain: Why Students' Unions Are Acting Unlawfully - published by ISGAP(Institute for the Study of Global Antisemitism and Policy – February 2016.

Judged the Debating Matters Yorkshire Final Competition – Leeds, February 2016.

Paper delivered Indiana University's Institute for the Study of Contemporary Antisemitism Conference – Anti-Zionism, Antisemitism and the Dynamics of Delegitmization – *Fraser v The UCU: Anti-Zionism, Antisemitism and Racializing Discourse* – April 2016. Spent June developing this paper into an 8,000 word chapter.

Paper delivered at the 74th Mid-Western Political Science Conference in Chicago – *Jeremy Corbyn: Why the British Labour Party is No Longer a Safe Place for Jews* – April 2016

Paper delivered at the Genocide and Human Rights in Comparative Perspective Confernece at Kalamazoo College, Michigan – *Legacies of the Holocaust: Denials and Other Distortions.* I also acted as a 'discussant' (commentator on other people's papers) at this conference.

Paper delivered at the Israel Academia Monitor Conference, Tel Aviv University – *Lessons Learned from Fraser v The UCU* – May 2016.

Assisted student taking an appeal against a decision by his university to dismiss his complaint of antisemitic harassment to the OIA (Office of the Independent Adjudicator) on behalf of UKLFI (UK Lawyers for Israel). (I worked with another lawyer on the case and this case had been ongoing since June 2014

and I had been involved in the case since then, helping to draft documents, etc.)
Submitted evidence to the Shami Chakrabarti Inquiry – June 2016.

Howard Jacobson

An award-winning writer and broadcaster, Howard Jacobson was born in Manchester and brought up in Prestwich. He studied at Downing College, Cambridge under F. R. Leavis. He lectured for three years at the University of Sydney before returning to teach at Selwyn College, Cambridge.

His novels include The Mighty Walzer and Zoo Time, each winners of the Bollinger Everyman Wodehouse Prize, Kalooki Nights, longlisted for the Man Booker Prize and the 2010 Man Booker Prize-winning The Finkler Question.

Bibliography
Fiction
Coming From Behind, Chatto & Windus, 1983
Peeping Tom, Chatto & Windus, 1984
Redback, Bantam, 1986

The Very Model of a Man, Viking, 1992
No More Mister Nice Guy, Cape, 1998
The Mighty Walzer, Cape, 1999
Who's Sorry Now?, Cape, 2002
The Making of Henry, Cape, 2004
<u>*Kalooki Nights*</u>, Cape, 2006
The Act of Love, Cape, 2008
<u>*The Finkler Question*</u>, Bloomsbury, 2010
Zoo Time, Bloomsbury, 2012
J, Bloomsbury 2014 (shortlisted for the 2014
Man Booker Prize
Shylock Is My Name: a novel, Hogarth 2016
Pussy: a novel, Cape, April 13, 2017 .

Non-fiction
*Shakespeare's Magnanimity: Four Tragic
Heroes, Their Friends and Families* (co-author
with Wilbur Sanders), Chatto & Windus, 1978
In the Land of Oz, Hamish Hamilton, 1987
Roots Schmoots: Journeys Among Jews, Viking,
1993
*Seriously Funny: From the Ridiculous to the
Sublime*, Viking, 1997
Whatever It Is, I Don't Like It, Bloomsbury,
2011

Owen Power

Is a life-long campaigner for equality. He worked for many years as a training manager delivering skills training to people with disabilities. He served as an equality advisor for a range of social projects and produced an audio cassette for people without sight on safer sex & HIV/AIDS awareness for World AIDS Day 1992. In 2001 Owen started to study at the Centre for Jewish Studies University of Manchester. His qualifications include BA (Hons), MA in Jewish Studies and MPhil. His thesis on the Jewish thinker Hugh Schonfield was published in 2013 by Wipf & Stock. Owen is a member of the Manchester Liberal shul and serves as a social action officer; he is also a volunteer with the Manchester LGBT Foundation and a member of the Labour Party.

Stephen Spencer Ryde

focuses his personal time on addressing the lack of balance in the media, the ignorance and stereotyping of Jews, defending Israel against unjust condemnation and challenging the growing trend of antisemitism. He writes in media, works with StandWithUs and attends anti Israel / antisemitic events covertly to expose hatred. He campaigns tirelessly in the defence of Jews and the Jewish State and works to increase awareness of the threats that confront Jews here in the UK.

Noru Tsalic
Born and raised a Communist regime, Noru has studied, lived and worked in Romania, Israel and the United Kingdom. He has served both in the Romanian Army and the Israel Defence Forces. His diverse upbringing has taught him the value of liberal democracy, but has also imparted understanding and respect for different cultures, ideologies and points of view.
Noru is very proud of his Jewish heritage and culture. In the United Kingdom, he has become an active member of the British Jewish community -- he has, for instance, served on the Executive Committee of the Coventry Reform Jewish Community. Like for the vast majority of Jews, Israel is an essential part of Noru's national, religious and cultural identity.

235

Having studied Chemical Engineering and
Business Administration, Noru is currently a
management consultant. In his spare time, he
writes political blogs, participates in debates
and reads avidly. He is often invited to deliver
presentations on issues related to Israel and to
the Middle East in general.

Jonathan Turner
is a barrister practising in intellectual property
and competition law in London. He has acted
in a number of leading cases in this area and is
the author of the textbook "Intellectual
Property and EU Competition Law" (2nd Ed,
OUP, 2015) and other publications in this
fields. He is a Panellist of the World
Intellectual Property Organisation and the
Czech Arbitration Court for domain name
disputes, and he served as an elected Director
of the Authors' Licensing and Collecting
Society from 2010 to 2016. In 2011 he and
several other lawyers founded the voluntary
association, UK Lawyers for Israel, which he
now chairs.

Judy Weleminsky
is the Founder of Pro Israel, Pro Palestinian, Pro Peace and promotes engagement with ordinary people on the streets combatting the hatred of the so called Pro Palestinian Campaigners. Judy spent her working life in the voluntary sector promoting the rights of minorities, of people with mental health problems and in leadership roles of national community and mental health charities. Judy was an active local member of the Labour party for almost 30 years and resigned in 2004

Plus Extracts from:

House of Commons Home Affairs Committee, Antisemitism in the UK October 2016

A History of the Jews, Paul Johnson, Weidenfeld and Nicholson